Revise for Geography GCSE OCR Specification A

David Atkins

Heinemann Educational Publishers
Halley Court
Jordan Hill
Oxford
OX2 8EJ

Part of Harcourt Education

Heinemann is the registered trade mark of
Harcourt Education Limited

Text © David Atkins

First published 2000
Second edition 2002

06 05 04
10 9 8 7 6 5 4 3 2

British Library Cataloguing in Publication Data
A catalogue record for this book is available from the British Library

ISBN 0 435 09971 X

Designed, typeset and illustrated by Magnet Harlequin, Oxford

Printed and bound in the UK by Bath Colour Books

Acknowledgements

Maps and extracts
pp.13, 30 David Waugh *Wider World*, 1980, Nelson Thornes; p.26, 27 *Key Geography for GCSE Teachers Resource Guide*, Nelson Thornes; pp.31, 104, 105, 106 and 107 Maps reproduced from Ordnance Survey mapping with the permission of The Controller of Her Majesty's Stationery Office © Crown copyright. All rights reserved. Licence no. 100000230; p.44 David Waugh *The New Wider World*, 1998, Nelson Thornes; p54 © GMPTE, 1999, Manchester; pp 67, 69 ed Flinders, *A New Introduction to Geography*, Hodder & Stoughton Educational, a division of HodderHeadline plc; pp. 80, 81 Victoria Bishop and Peter Prosser *The Environment*, Collins Educational.

Photographs
p.44 Centro; p.43 Environmental Images; p.82 Panos/David Reed; p101 Aerofilms.

The author would like to thank:
British Army, Brierley Hill Library, British Coal, Environment Agency, National Power, Nottinghamshire County Council, OCR Exam Board and the Office for National Statistics.

The publishers have made every effort to trace the copyright holders. However if any material has been overlooked or incorrectly acknowledged, we would be pleased to correct this at the earliest opportunity.

Tel: 01865 888058 www.heinemann.co.uk

Contents

Introduction

How to use this book

Welcome to the Heinemann Revision Guide for OCR specification A and let me start with a challenge: **think how many more opportunities there will be in your life if you can raise five of your subjects by just one grade**. This revision guide helps you to achieve that objective in geography.

Geography is one of the most varied and interesting subjects, covering dramatic events such as earthquakes and volcanic eruptions and awe-inspiring features found along our changing coastlines. It also includes environmental issues such as global warming and everyday features that we see around us, such as towns and shops. All these have an impact on us and we can have an impact on them.

Specification A

This specification includes coursework (worth 25% of the final grade), which is not covered in this book. There are two exams. Papers 1 and 2 (50%) deal mainly with knowledge, understanding, its application and some skills. Papers 3 and 4 (25%) cover skills and the *application* of understanding, but there is an overlap between the two. For both exams there is a choice of two levels – a foundation tier (C–G) and a higher tier (grades A*–D).

Paper 1 is the foundation paper and contains the four units shown in this guide. One question is provided for each unit – so there is no choice. Paper 2 is the higher tier exam. Two questions are provided for each unit and candidates choose one from each unit. Paper 3 (foundation) and Paper 4 (higher tier) both have two questions in which there is no choice. Therefore, whichever exam you enter you will need to have a widespread knowledge covering all four sections. You cannot learn everything on, for example, volcanoes and hope to pass. This revision guide is laid out so the four units can be clearly identified and understood.

Throughout each unit in this book the questions used are *extracted* from actual exam questions. Take the time to do these questions and then look at the answers in the back. See where you answered incorrectly, but also look where you missed marks through lack of explanation.

Ponder carefully the comments and advice given. Losing 5 marks per question will cost you at least one grade, so be positive and win those extra 5 marks each time.

Even this revision guide can only assist you in preparing for your exam. It cannot do the work for you. However, you can plan for success by *learning your named examples* (or case studies). ***This is the key to success in this exam.*** In any past exam paper roughly 7 marks out of every 19 are based on the 'named examples'. For this new specification 5 marks will be available for each case study on the Foundation paper and 7 on the Higher Level paper. If you learn the detail of the relevant examples that apply to the features being tested (which are listed in the specification), you are well on the way to achieving a high mark. If you do not learn the named example your teacher gives, you will struggle. See page 6 for details of how case studies are marked.

Hints and Tips!
Passing an exam has very little to do with luck – you must be prepared to work.

Specimen question and answer

The Exam Board expects you to **explain** your answers and marks are allocated for this purpose. In this sample answer the main answer gains one mark and the two reasons that follow increase the marks.

Hints and Tips!
Take control of the revision process and plan intelligently.

'Explain why the Meadowhall Shopping Centre in Sheffield was built on a site located outside the city centre.'

A good answer would include the following: 'Meadowhall was built on the site of an old steelworks (1 mark), which meant the land was cheap (1 mark) and there was plenty of space available (1 mark)'.

Notice how the main answer gains one mark and the two explanations that follow triple the final mark (see page 6).

Read each word of the question carefully. Look for the trigger words. If the question says 'What are the effects of earthquakes?' then the trigger words are *effects* and *earthquakes*. Don't waste time writing about the causes of earthquakes. You will not get any marks if you do not answer the question given.

Reread page 4 and realise that you should try not to drift into the exam.

If the question refers to an EU example, *do not* use the UK. The exam writer wants to test your knowledge beyond the UK.

Avoid using Norway or Switzerland as examples of an EU country. They are not EU members and you will not gain full marks if you use them.

Revising actively

Throughout the book there are hints and tips to improve your revision and examination technique. Special notes are included on the right hand side of most of the pages in the book. You have already come across some of these:

Extra information and useful facts and ideas to help you with your examination answers.

Hints and Tips! These give general advice and useful information to help you prepare for and sit the examination. Following the advice could stop you wasting time and improve your grade.

Things to do: boxes to tick to check your progress, gaps to fill in, activities to focus your revision to improve your grade. If you do well, be pleased with yourself. If at first you don't do well, re-read the section and test yourself again.

All the chapters include some practice questions similar to those you will face in the examination. Each question includes the number of marks you can hope to achieve. Page 112 onwards give mark schemes for the test questions and lots of other useful advice on the best way to answer questions – and even how not to answer them!

Good luck. Work hard, but...
- Try to enjoy your revision. It should be satisfying to see the whole subject come together at the end of the course. You become a real geographer and real geographers impress examiners.
- Plan your revision carefully. Be methodical and work steadily. Desperate last minute cramming leads to panic!

Hints and Tips!
If you do not work effectively you cannot hope to succeed.

Revision advice

- Plan your revision. Begin several months before the exam by going over the main points. In the final few weeks it is worth identifying the specific details you still have to learn. Use the chart overleaf to plan the last few weeks' revision for all your subjects.
- Revise for about 45 minutes then take a short break for the brain to absorb all the facts. Then (and this is the hard bit) come back for another 45-minute session. Don't allow your short break to last 45 minutes!
- Before learning new material review what you learned earlier. Then review it again one day, one week and one month later. Using this method your brain is working in its most effective way. For many people revising and reviewing information five or six times really locks the facts into the brain.
- Many people find mind maps, spider or flow diagrams, codes and rhymes helpful ways to revise. Examples of these are found in this revision guide, but the best ones are those you devise for yourself.
- Don't believe that just reading this guide is revising – it isn't. Follow the exercises and don't cheat!
- Finally, don't attempt to learn two years' work in one evening. All the best advice is to work in manageable chunks, a bit at a time.
- Take control of your revision process. Realise the value of named examples, understand and learn the process involved, learn the proper names and understand the key ideas.

Work hard and intelligently and we trust you will be successful in all your exams.

Levels marking

Many answers and all case studies will in future be marked according to the principle of levels. It is vital that you grasp now what will be expected of you during the exams so that you can properly prepare yourself.

Marks will be awarded according to the quality of your answer not the number of points you make. If a question has seven marks do not expect to gain full marks by giving seven vague answers even if they are all correct. Look at the examples below to see what is required.

Question 1

Name and locate a coastal feature formed by deposition. Describe it and explain how it was formed. Draw a labelled diagram as part of your answer. (6 marks.)

A Level 1 answer (gaining 1–3 marks) might include a poorly drawn diagram and a description of a spit or an explanation of longshore drift.

A Level 2 answer (gaining 4–6 marks) would include a diagram and a description of a spit and an explanation of longshore drift.

A Level 3 answer (gaining a maximum of 5 marks for the Foundation (Paper 1) and 7 marks for the Higher (Paper 2), see also page 4) would include a named example, e.g. Hurst Castle in Hampshire, a clear and labelled diagram (perhaps like the one on p.29), a description of the formation of a spit due to longshore drift, *and* would go further and refer to the influence of the wind in altering the shape of the spit (recurving) and the build up of salt marshes behind the spit.

Note: that if you draw your diagram first it makes it a lot easier to describe the processes. You have something to refer to whilst writing your answer.

The need for clear labelled diagrams should also encourage you to draw good maps and diagrams in your exercise book during your GCSE studies.

Question 2

Look at this second example.

'Describe the effects of an earthquake in a named area on people and the local economy.' (7 marks)

Answers that only mentioned falling buildings, fire, damaged roads and people being killed would not win more than 3 marks.

Answers that referred to the type of building that collapsed, the number of deaths, gas pipes fracturing causing fires and the disruption to local firms for many months are more precise and detailed so would achieve the *Level 2* range of marks (4–6).

It is only one more step to get the opportunity of full marks by providing a named example, e.g. Los Angeles in California. If you can also mention specific named details, e.g. it was the Santa Monica bridge that collapsed, it would also help.

Often you need to give a named example to gain the highest mark. The summary section at the end of each unit gives you the chance to identify and learn these.

Question 3

Consider this last example:

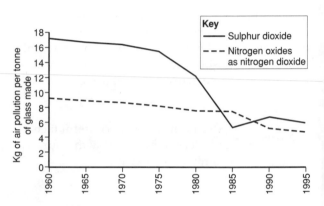

'Since 1965 the glass industry has tried to reduce air pollution. Use the evidence from the diagram to describe how successful it has been.' (6 marks)

Here the answers are actually provided for you on the graph! An answer that simply said pollution was going down deserves only 1 mark. To gain 6 marks here you need to describe the trends *quoting the figures on the graph* and referring to the slight rise between 1985 and 1990.

Do not be put off if you have only just started your course and do not know some of the answers given above. If *Level 3* looks hard do not despair but gradually build up your expertise during your time in years 10 and 11. Do not leave it till the last minute.

Quality of written work

Up to four marks in Papers 1 and 2 and two marks in Papers 3 and 4 are awarded for the quality of your written work. Spelling, grammar, punctuation, sentence composition and correct use of geographical terms are all taken into account. Again try to build up the quality of your work in Key Stage 4.

Unit 1: People and the physical world

Exam Watch

This unit covers the reasons why earthquakes and volcanoes happen, and a study of where they are located. The behaviour of rivers and their impact on the landscape forms the second section. The last part looks at Britain's changing coastline, including the dramatic features caused by erosion and deposition. As well as learning the facts, you need to be aware of the interaction between the physical landscape and human activity. People alter the way the physical processes work – sometimes with disastrous results.

Candidates in the higher paper answer *one* of the two questions provided. Candidates in the foundation paper have only one question provided.

Plate tectonics

Key ideas
- The distribution of earthquakes and volcanoes is related to plate margins.
- What are the causes and effects of earthquakes and volcanic eruptions?
- Why do people live in areas where the earth is unstable?
- How do people respond to an earthquake or volcanic eruption?

Hints and Tips!

Learn to use the key words wherever possible.

Key words and definitions

Destructive (convergent) margin	where one plate moves under the other and is destroyed.
Divergent (constructive) margin	where two plates move away from each other.
Inertia	this means at rest. In this section it refers to people who do not want to move. They are happy where they are.
Liquefaction	ground turning to a liquid state as water is shaken up from below.
Magma	molten rock, gas and steam.
Plate margins	where two plates meet.
Plates	large areas of land and sea bed. Each plate is moving slowly.
Subduction zone	the area where one plate is dragged under the other.
Transform margin	where two plates slide past each other and no material is destroyed.

This is a fascinating topic, partly because of the drama and colour of a volcanic eruption and partly because of the unbelievably powerful forces at work. Sadly, earthquakes and volcanoes can bring death and destruction, which should not be forgotten. This unit studies how people come to terms with earthquakes and volcanic eruptions and turn them to their own advantage.

Look at Figure 1.1 showing the structure of the earth.

Surrounding the solid core of the earth is the mantle, a very hot area where rocks are in a semi-molten state. Finally comes the outer layer called the crust, which is broken up into very large chunks of land and sea bed called plates. These plates move very slowly (2–3 cm a year), giving us our present-day pattern of continents.

▼ Figure 1.1 Structure of the Earth

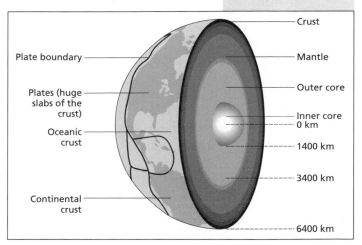

Plate boundary — Crust

Plates (huge slabs of the crust) — Mantle

Oceanic crust — Outer core

Continental crust — Inner core
0 km
1400 km
3400 km
6400 km

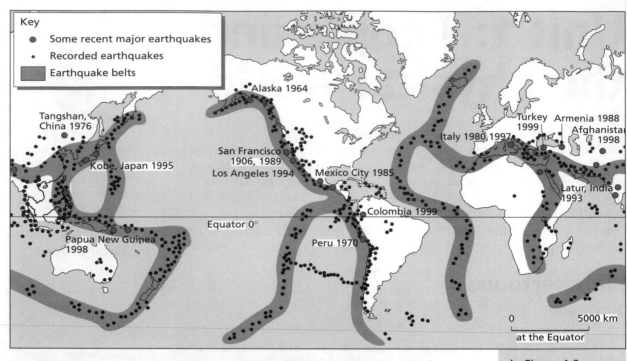

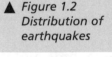

Figure 1.2
Distribution of
earthquakes

Distribution of earthquakes and volcanoes

Carefully study Figures 1.2 and 1.3. It is immediately obvious that
earthquakes and volcanoes happen in certain regions and not in others.
Also, earthquakes and volcanoes both occur in the same regions. Why is
this?

If you crack (but do not remove) the shell of a hard-boiled egg, you will
understand the situation of the earth, with large and small pieces of shell
representing the earth's plates. A city or country that is not near the *edge* of
the plate will rarely be affected by earthquakes. It is near where the plates
join (the **plate margins**) that the action happens.

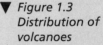

Figure 1.3
Distribution of
volcanoes

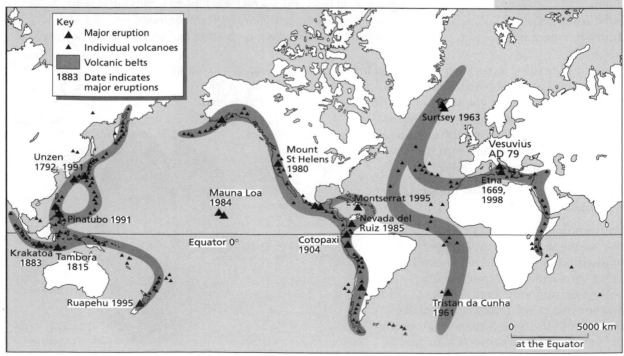

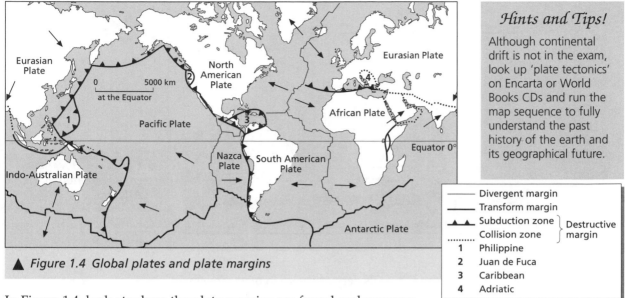

Hints and Tips!

Although continental drift is not in the exam, look up 'plate tectonics' on Encarta or World Books CDs and run the map sequence to fully understand the past history of the earth and its geographical future.

——	Divergent margin
——	Transform margin
▲▲▲	Subduction zone } Destructive
....	Collision zone } margin
1	Philippine
2	Juan de Fuca
3	Caribbean
4	Adriatic

▲ *Figure 1.4 Global plates and plate margins*

In Figure 1.4, look at where the plate margins are found and compare them with the location of volcanoes and earthquakes. What do you notice?

Where are there eruptions *not* explained by plate margins?

You don't have to learn any of the above maps. **You do need to know about one earthquake and one volcanic eruption in detail** – why they happened and how people reacted to them.

It is vital to realise and understand why the plate margins, earthquakes and volcano belts all occur in the same regions of the world. It is the movement of plates along the margins that causes the earthquakes and volcanoes. The whole jigsaw pattern has only been properly understood since the 1960s, and so it is a new and exciting 'science'.

Divergent (constructive) margins

Here two plates move away from each other (by about 4–5 cm a year). Molten lava from below rises up and seals the gap, then becomes new solid land. Hence new land is constructed. Later that solid rock is pulled apart by the movement of the plates and so the process continues.

An example is the situation under the Atlantic. South America and Africa were once joined (look at the shape of both). Slowly they have moved away from each other.

Stop and Think

You may have visited Tenerife, Lanzarote or Gran Canaria. These are all volcanic islands formed by plate movement.

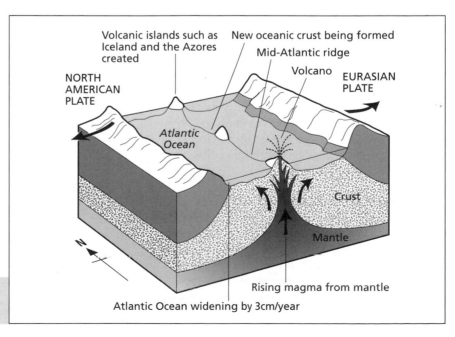

► *Figure 1.5 The mid-Atlantic divergent margin*

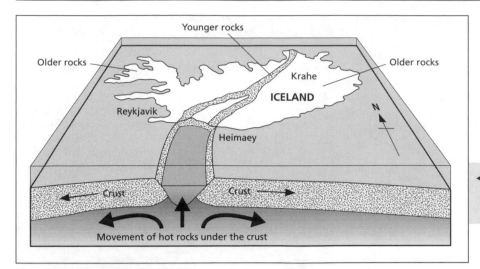

Figure 1.6 How new crust is created in the Atlantic

Iceland stands on a plate margin and owes its very existence to plate movement.

Figure 1.6 shows how the centre of the island is fairly young and the outer edges are older. If the plates had never moved Iceland would not exist. Under the Atlantic is a long range of mountains running north to south. Earthquake and volcanic activity is quite mild in such circumstances. Logically, if new material is being made and the earth gets no bigger, then somewhere material must be destroyed.

Destructive (convergent) margins

These are where a plate is destroyed as two plates move together and collide. This will happen at the *subduction* or *collision* zone. The heavier oceanic plate is dragged down and destroyed by the friction between the two plates and by the heat of the mantle below. The material is then recycled upwards to form volcanoes. As the oceanic plate is dragged down it jolts. Each jolt causes an earthquake. So, destructive plate margins, earthquakes and volcanoes all occur in the same general area. Notice the deep trench created where the plate begins its downward journey.

Collision zones

Again, this is where two continental crust plates collide but here material from the collision is pushed upwards, forming mountains. Look in an atlas and see how the Alps lie at 90° to Italy, which collided with Europe long ago. India is still colliding with Asia and forming the Himalayas even today. Notice the angle of these mountains to India. Earthquakes are associated with this collision, such as that at Latur, India, 1993.

Transform (conservative) margins

Some textbooks call these conservative margins as the plates are not created or destroyed. This is where two plates jolt their way past each other. The plates lock together until the friction is overcome by the sheer power of the forces that drive them. Each jolt causes an earthquake movement.

Figure 1.7 The South American destructive margin

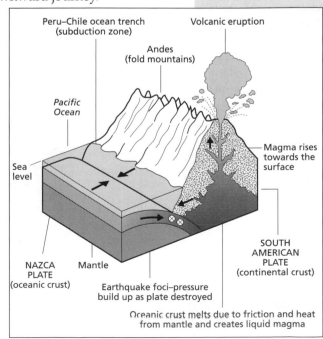

Earthquakes

In California (on the west side of the United States), the Pacific Plate should be travelling north west at 5cm per year faster than the American Plate. In 1906 an earthquake destroyed the centre of San Francisco, causing more than 450 deaths and destroying at least 25,000 buildings. The ground had moved by 6 metres! Since 1906 the two plates have remained locked together but pressure has been steadily building up for what many people predict will be 'the big one'. A few people think that the earthquake in 1989 was the 'the big one', while others say that the two plates will ease themselves past each other section by section. Every Californian is aware that San Francisco and Los Angeles could be destroyed in a massive earthquake but he or she chooses to stay.

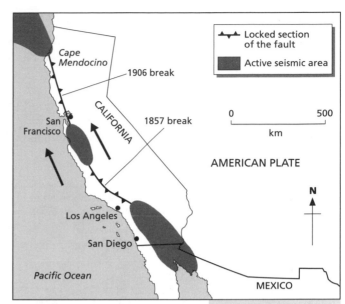

▲ Figure 1.8 The San Andreas fault and California earthquakes – an example of a transform plate margin.

The number of people who die in earthquakes depends partly on the wealth of the country concerned, the level of technology available, whether the earthquake strikes in rural or urban areas, and whether it happens during the day, at night or at rush hour.

Know your case study

San Francisco Earthquake, 1906 and 1989

The North American Plate and the Pacific Plates had been locked together, but in April 1906 the plates in the San Francisco area suddenly moved by 6 metres. The earthquake measured 8.2 on the Richter Scale.

- Many buildings collapsed and several bridges were damaged.
- Gas and water pipes fractured as the ground moved.
- *Initially*, there were few deaths.
- *However*, as sparks ignited the gas escaping from pipes, fire swept through the town centre. 450 people died and more than 25,000 buildings were destroyed.
- Much of central San Francisco was built on sand. The shaking of the ground brought water to the surface, making the sand very unstable. This is called *liquefaction*. Many buildings just tilted over.
- Before long the city was rebuilt – in its old location.
- By comparison the San Francisco earthquake of 1989 was 6.9 on the Richter Scale and the ground moved by 1.2 metres. This time 63 people were killed and far fewer properties destroyed because of greater knowledge about earthquake-proof building and also valves on the gas pipes reduced the number of gas escapes.
- The double-deck Bay Bridge collapsed because of inadequate construction standards and fire destroyed many wooden buildings in the Marina district. This area was constructed on land created from the rubble of the 1906 earthquake!

Hints and Tips!

You need to learn the details of one earthquake and one volcano. Make sure you pick an example that shows the reason for the feature, what happened on the day, and what the effects were. Careful choice of examples is important. Learn also the effects on the local people.

Why do people stay in known earthquake and volcano zones?

1. Lived there all their life. Inertia – too much trouble to move.
2. People are often fatalistic – willing to take their chances.
3. Jobs and family are local. These are big incentives to stay.
4. Some are too poor to move.
5. California, for example, has a mild climate – good for farming – and is a pleasant place to live.
6. Many trust technology in the belief that scientists will warn them in time (see Figure 1.9).

Hints and Tips!

This is perhaps the most frequently asked question over the past ten years! Make sure you can give detailed answers. See also page 14 and check your own notes and textbooks.

Test Yourself

List five reasons why people stay in potential earthquake zones.

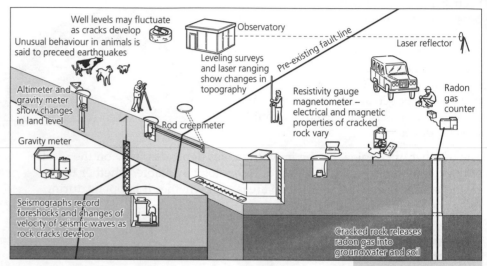

Well levels may fluctuate as cracks develop

Unusual behaviour in animals is said to preceed earthquakes

Observatory

Leveling surveys and laser ranging show changes in topography

Pre-existing fault-line

Laser reflector

Altimeter and gravity meter show changes in land level

Gravity meter

Rod creepmeter

Resistivity gauge magnetometer – electrical and magnetic properties of cracked rock vary

Radon gas counter

Seismographs record foreshocks and changes of velocity of seismic waves as rock cracks develop

Cracked rock releases radon gas into groundwater and soil

▲ Figure 1.9 Measuring earth movement

Preparing for an earthquake

Economically advanced countries such as the USA and Japan can prepare for earthquakes in ways that poor countries cannot always copy. These methods include:

1. Investing in monitoring equipment to warn of approaching earthquakes (see Fig 1.9).
2. Building earthquake-proof buildings which sway with the earthquake and absorb its energy. Remember the Trans America building in your textbook. Compare it to the single-storey mud buildings in India and Turkey which tend to collapse on the occupants and kill them straight away.
3. Earthquake drills – so the people do not panic during an earthquake but stay in safe places (e.g. under a desk).
4. Education – so people have fresh water, torches, radios and telephone numbers of relatives ready for when an earthquake happens.
5. Ensuring public water supplies are available for several days by building earthquake-proof water tanks and installing shut off valves to prevent loss of water from damaged pipes.

Know your case study

Richter Scale

Earthquakes can be measured according to the *effect* they have. The Richter Scale runs from 0 to 10. Each level is ten times more powerful than the one below.
The most powerful earthquake recorded so far reached 8.9.

0	
1 2	Normally only detected by seismometers
3 4	Moderate vibration
5	Strong vibration. Objects fall off shelves.
6	Walls crack.
7	Buildings collapse.
8	Towns destroyed.
9 10	Total devastation.

Questions

The power of an earthquake can be measured by the Richter Scale. Look at Figure 1.10 and suggest:

(a) Why the Indian earthquake at only 6.0 led to more deaths than the San Francisco earthquake at 6.9.

(b) Why the Kobe earthquake at 7.2 led to more deaths than the Romanian earthquake at 7.5.

Tip: If you need help answering the questions, look back over this chapter and your own notes.

Hints and Tips!

This is an example of a scatter graph – one of the graphs you need to understand.

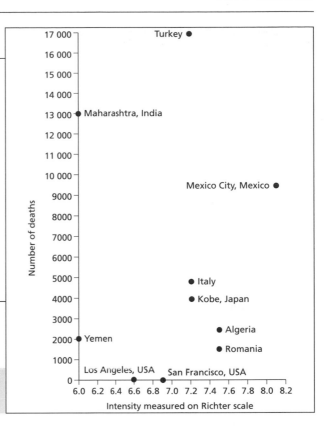

▶ Figure 1.10 Comparing earthquakes

Volcanoes

As shown earlier in Figure 1.7, there is a strong connection between the location of plate margins and volcanoes. If there were no plate movements, then few if any volcanoes would exist. The magma beneath the crust is under great pressure and so wherever there is a weakness in the crust the magma will try to force its way through from time to time.

Hints and Tips!

Remember that you need to know the details of one volcanic eruption.

Know your case study

Mount St Helens – 18 May 1980

There are minute-by-minute accounts of this dramatic eruption because of video footage of the event, which you have probably seen. Do not get overwhelmed by the detail but have clear in your mind the causes, the main events of that day and the consequences. You need to describe and explain what happened to gain your 7 marks.

▼ Figure 1.11 The eruption of Mount St Helens

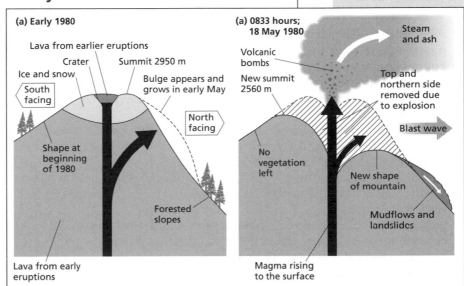

Case study *continued*

Basic causes

The Juan de Fuca Plate is being driven under the west coast of the North American Plate. As it goes down it melts and the lighter material forces its way up through the North America Plate and from time to time bursts out onto the surface creating the volcanic cone. The main vent inside Mount St Helens had cooled and become blocked. This is a crucial fact to understand.

Events

During early 1980 pressure began building up within the volcano. There were several minor earthquakes and eruptions. Because of the blocked main vent a bulge had developed on the side of the volcano.

Then on 18 May:

- An earthquake occurred which caused the bulge to move.
- A landslide of mud, ice and snow moved downhill.
- Spirit Lake was filled by the landslide creating a mudflow further downstream.
- The removal of the ice and rock allowed the very hot magma to explode sideways, totally destroying half of the cone.

Effects

- Trees within 10 miles were blasted to the ground.
- All life was destroyed including 61 people who died despite warnings.
- Ash was deposited over a huge area – even as far as the east coast of America.
- Crops, coated with the ash, were ruined.
- Roads, bridges and houses were destroyed.
- Later, however, it became a **tourist attraction** in its own right. Many thousands come bringing the usual mixed blessings of this leisure activity.

Why do people live near volcanoes?

- After an eruption the volcanic lava and the dust weather down to provide very fertile soils. This attracts farmers.
- Following the publicity surrounding the eruption in Mt St Helens in 1980, there has been a great upturn in tourists who want to see the site for themselves. Many jobs connected with tourism have grown in number.
- Tenerife is a very popular holiday destination, noted for its scenery, beaches and sunshine. A volcanic island, Tenerife owes its existence to plate movement near the Mid-Atlantic Ridge.
- As the magma cools down in the vent, the minerals sometimes arrange themselves to form diamonds. This creates many jobs, from mining to the jewellery trade.
- Increased satellite observations and a greater understanding of the behaviour of volcanoes, linked to better warning systems, help the people to feel safer near active volcanoes.
- Geothermal energy (heat from the magma) can sometimes be used. Often the best sites are near volcanoes, e.g. in New Zealand and Iceland.

Test Yourself

List five reasons why people stay in earthquake zones. Then check on page 12.

- Volcanic eruptions can sometimes be spotted before they happen. This gives time for people to escape.
- Volcanoes create steep sides suitable for skiing. The ski lift was a casualty in the 2001 Mt Etna eruption in Italy.

Questions

Look at Figure 1.12 and explain why the plate margin is some distance from the line of the volcanoes that runs from north to south almost parallel to the plate margin.

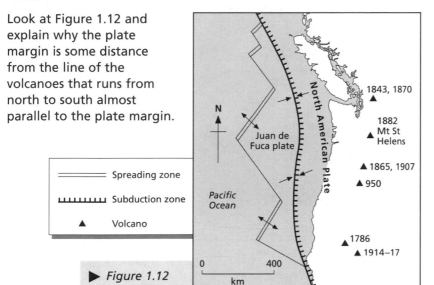

Spreading zone

Subduction zone

▲ Volcano

▶ Figure 1.12

After the Nyiragongo volcano erupted in the Congo, 200,000 refugees returned to the town of Goma whilst the lava was still cooling! There was no other place to go which had clean water. They did not want to live in refugee camps for the rest of their lives.

Examination Practice Questions – higher level paper

Answer sections (a) and (b) and take about 15 minutes. Check your answers at the back then answer section (c); again take about 15 minutes.

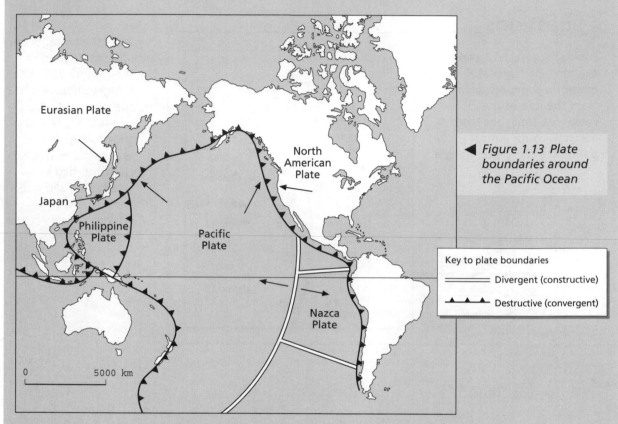

◀ *Figure 1.13 Plate boundaries around the Pacific Ocean*

(a) Use information from Figure 1.13 to explain why there are earthquakes in Japan. [5]

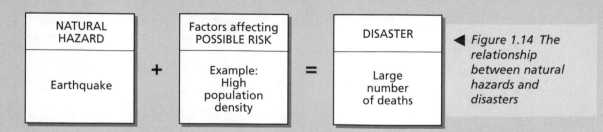

◀ *Figure 1.14 The relationship between natural hazards and disasters*

(b) Study Figure 1.14.

Why do many people continue to live in cities that are at risk from earthquakes? You may refer to examples that you have studied. [7]

(c) For a named volcano that you have studied:

(i) Explain the causes of the volcanic eruption. You may draw a diagram or diagrams as part of your answer. [3]

(ii) Describe how the volcanic eruption affected the surrounding area. [4]

[Total 19 marks]

Examination Practice Question – foundation level paper

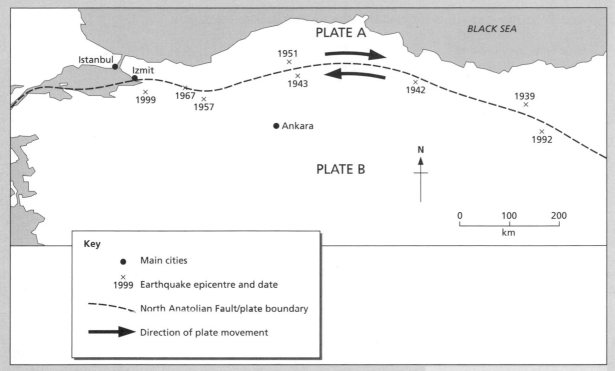

▲ Figure 1.15
Earthquake activity in
northern Turkey 1939–99

(a) (i) Describe the movement of plates A and B along the North Anatolian Fault.
(Clue: look at the years and work out in which direction the earth activity is moving.) [1]

(ii) Explain why the earthquake activity occurs along plate boundaries such as the North
Anatolian Fault. (Clue: use what you know about California's situation and adapt it to
fit this example. It is the same process.) [2]

(b) Describe three ways by which the effects of earthquakes could be reduced. [3]

(c) Why do many people still live where earthquakes occur? [3]

(d) Describe the effects of either the earthquake in Turkey or another earthquake you have
studied. Study page 6 to achieve a high level answer. [5]

Hints and Tips!

In your exam you will
come across several maps
and diagrams you have
not seen before in your
textbooks. This is one of
them. Do not be alarmed.
The ideas and processes
are just the same.

Hints and Tips!

Be ready to identify and
mention anomalies (facts
that do not fit the
pattern). The 1992
earthquake is the anomaly
here. Do not let anomalies
upset your understanding
of the main processes.

Hints and Tips!

Do not stay with the
exam example unless you
can answer it well. This is
your chance to give an
example you know well –
San Francisco or Kobe in
Japan or whatever
example you have studied
in school. Ensure you
describe the effects and
not the causes.

Note: this is an *extract* from a question. So the marks do not total 19, as they would for a full question.

Rivers

Key ideas
- Water flows in a cycle from the clouds to the sea and back to the clouds.
- Rivers erode, transport and deposit material and cause distinctive features in the landscape.
- Flooding can sometimes be controlled by human activity and sometimes made worse by it.

Key words and definitions

Basin	the area containing all the streams and watercourses of one river.
Deposition	where material is put down.
Erosion	the wearing away and removal of material.
Evapotranspiration	where trees and plants take water out of the soil and pass it into the air, combined with the effects of evaporation from leaves and the ground itself.
Flood plain	area flooded when a river bursts its banks.
Meanders	bends in the river.
Overland flow	water moving on the surface towards the river.
Saturation	when the ground is so full of water it cannot take in any more.
Watershed	a line along the top of a range of hills which mark out the boundary of one basin, separating it from the next basin.

The hydrological cycle
Rivers and lakes can be thought of in the form of a system, as shown in Figure 1.16.

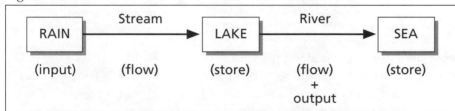

Hints and Tips!

Be ready for a question on *global* water stores and transfers.

◀ *Figure 1.16 River system*

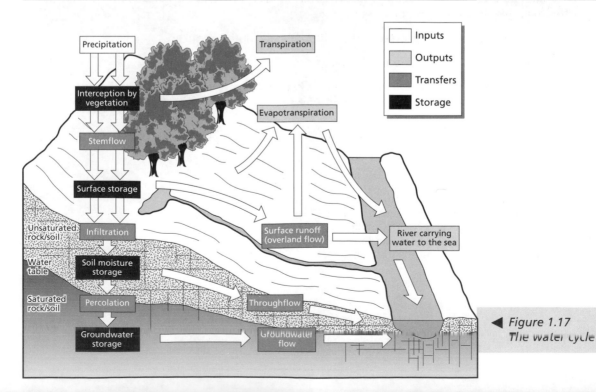

◀ *Figure 1.17 The water cycle*

Figure 1.16 shows that if people or the environment affect one part of the system there is a knock-on effect further along. A shortage of rain means reduced river flows and lower water levels in the lakes. Figure 1.17 shows the system in more detail. Try to understand the whole system.

Rain, snow etc. (**precipitation**) falls through the air; some reaches the ground but some is stopped (**intercepted**) by trees and buildings and later evaporates back into the air.

Water that reaches the ground may stay on the surface or soak in (**infiltrate**) and then move through the soil (**throughflow**) to reach the river. Some water moves down into the rocks below (**percolation**) and eventually through the rocks (**groundwater flow**) to rejoin the river. Trees absorb water out of the ground and release it out through the leaves. This is called **transpiration**. When it is combined with evaporation of water from the leaves and the ground it is called **evapotranspiration** – a long but useful word.

You also need to know about changes to the system. There are two in particular.

- **Question A.** What would happen if all the trees were removed?
- **Question B.** What would happen if the hillside were covered in tarmac?

The answers are similar: much more rain would reach the ground all at once. The ground might not be able to soak up all the water quickly, and so more would flow overland to the rivers. **Saturation** is where the soil has absorbed so much water that it is full and cannot take any more. If tarmac covered the ground the water would sit on the tarmac for longer, or flow on the surface to the river. In both cases there is an increased risk of flooding.

Questions on rivers and flooding appear in a number of ways – such as on a diagram, or on the map question, e.g. what would be the effect on the river of building a village at point X? It might be a photo question, e.g. label the feature (for example a forest) on the photo and say what effect its removal would have on the stream system. However the question comes, it will test your understanding of how the water flow changes. Often increased risk of flooding will be one aspect of the answer.

Examination Practice Question – foundation level paper (*extract only*)

Study the map in Figure 1.18 before looking at the questions overleaf (page 20).

Hints and Tips!

Learn the technical names for the processes and use them in the exam.

Hints and Tips!

A favourite question is to name three ways in which water reaches the river. What would you put as your answer?

▼ *Figure 1.18 Drainage basin of the River Torridge (in Devon)*

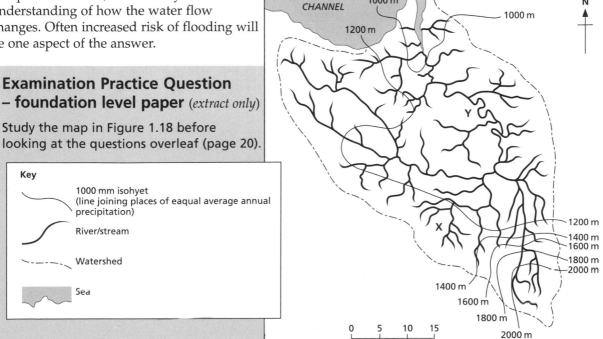

Key

~~~ 1000 mm isohyet (line joining places of eaqual average annual precipitation)

∿ River/stream

–·–·– Watershed

▨ Sea

Examination Practice Question – foundation level paper *continued*

- The river (with its tributary streams) flows north.

- The *watershed* marks the boundary of the river basin. All water that falls within this area will flow into the River Torridge.

- The isohyet lines show where most of the rain falls and by how much. This particular map shows that the rainfall is increasing as one travels south east.

(a) Shade the area with over 2000mm of rain.   [1]

(b) What would *cause* the increase of rainfall in the south east corner of the map?   [1]

(c) How will the volume of water in the river change as it flows from X to Y?   [1]

River erosion, transport and deposition processes

Erosion is the wearing away of material and features such as river banks. There are four words to learn here.

1. **Corrasion** – where the river hurls stones against the bank, weakening the material and later carrying it away
2. **Attrition** – stones are bounced against each other in the water and eventually break up
3. **Corrosion** – when salt and other chemicals in the river react with certain rocks in the landscape. (This is the same word and process that rusts cars.) The material is carried away in solution.
4. **Hydraulic pressure** – this is when the sheer force of the water momentarily traps air in the cracks, compressing the air and weakening the rock material, which then breaks and is carried away.

Hints and Tips!

1. These are the same four processes that are found in the sea, so learn them now and save yourself some revision effort.

2. The word CoACH can be used as a trigger in the exam room for these four processes. Try to devise your own mnemonic or trigger word for effective recall.

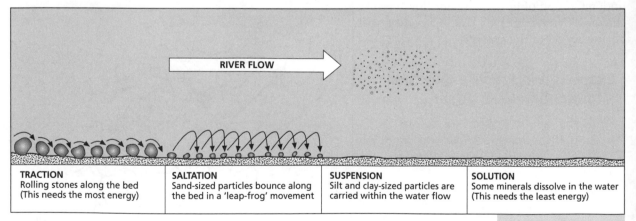

TRACTION	SALTATION	SUSPENSION	SOLUTION
Rolling stones along the bed (This needs the most energy)	Sand-sized particles bounce along the bed in a 'leap-frog' movement	Silt and clay-sized particles are carried within the water flow	Some minerals dissolve in the water (This needs the least energy)

Figure 1.19 shows how the eroded material is moved (transported). Learn **traction** and **saltation** in particular.

▲ *Figure 1.19 Process of transportation*

Deposition is where the river drops the eroded material as it lacks the energy to carry on transporting it. Naturally, large boulders are dropped first and the fine silt is deposited last, when the water is hardly flowing at all.

Landscapes produced by rivers

V-shaped valleys

In the mountains the river is cutting vertically downwards. Unstable soil leads to the 'V' shape of the actual valley, rather than a 'U' shape. If in doubt, remember Valley.

Interlocking spurs

In geography a spur is a slope sticking out from the main hillside. As the river flows down through the mountains it winds its way *around* pairs of these slopes, as shown in Figure 1.20.

Waterfalls

These occur where resistant hard rock is found together with weaker soft rock (see Figure 1.21). Not only is the soft rock below the waterfall eroded, but also the area below the hard rock at the back of the waterfall. This undercuts the overlying hard rock, which eventually breaks; the broken rocks fall into the plunge pool and the process starts all over again. The waterfall has thus moved a little further upstream. As one moves down the river towards the sea other features become more prominent. The river is now cutting laterally (sideways) or even depositing material, or both.

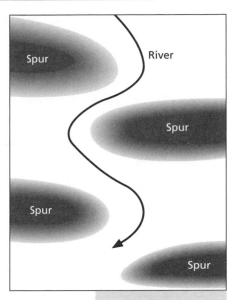

▲ Figure 1.20 Interlocking spurs

Waterfall retreats upstream
Valley side
Hard resistant rock
Softer, less resistant rock
Collapses
Overhang
Vertical gorge-like sides
Plunge pool
Undercutting
Fallen, angular rocks

◀ Figure 1.21 Formation of a waterfall

Hints and Tips!

Do not fall into the trap of writing that the *river* itself flows upstream!

Flood plains

Areas that flood if a river bursts its banks are called flood plains. In Figure 1.22 river B's valley will be more *extensively* flooded than river A's.

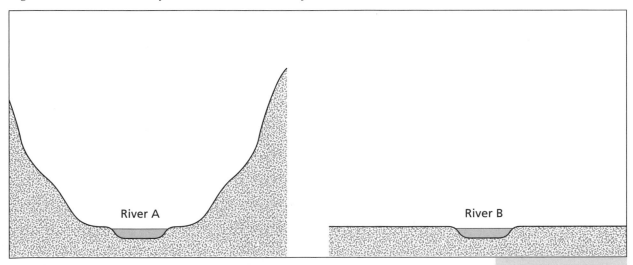

River A

River B

▲ Figure 1.22 Different types of floodplain

Clearly, with river B it would not be sensible to:
- build a house or village nearby (although 2 million British homes *are* on floodplains!)
- plant wheat – because it could be easily damaged by floodwater
- construct a major road nearby
- erect electric pylons near the river.

The land might be used for:
- grass which isn't damaged if it is frequently covered by water
- minor roads if the land doesn't flood often.

Levées

Levée is a French word meaning 'raised up'. It is used by geographers to describe how river banks are gradually built up when rivers flood, depositing coarse material on each side of the river channel. When the river is not in flood, material is deposited on the river bed itself. Slowly, both the river bed and the banks become progressively higher.

Hints and Tips!

The use of land near a river is a good guide to the frequency and likelihood of flooding. Use the points opposite as clues if there is a river question. Make sensible deductions.

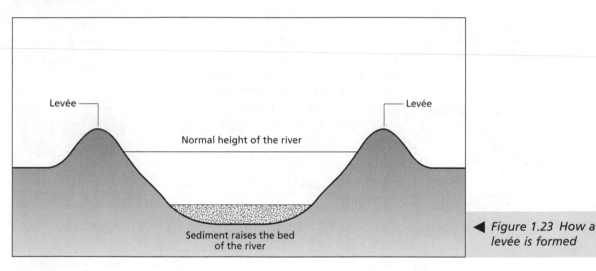

◀ *Figure 1.23 How a levée is formed*

Meanders

Meanders are bends in the river that can be very impressive and can be so large that towns develop within them (Shrewsbury and Durham are good examples). In the days when Britain was not as peaceful as it is now the river provided defence on three sides.

The key to understanding these features is that the river flows faster on the outside of the bend X and slower on the inside Y. Figure 1.24 shows the effect of this. On the left bank the faster-moving water erodes the soil, undercutting the otherwise near-vertical bank. On the right bank the water is moving more slowly and stones and silt are deposited. Over the years the whole river course will move from right to left. The water at point Z is flowing faster than all the rest as there is less friction there compared with the water touching the river bank and bed.

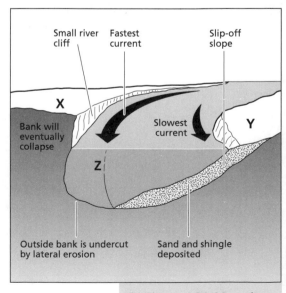

▲ *Figure 1.24 Meanders*

Ox-bow lakes

When the meanders become extremely tight ox-bow lakes may form. Figure 1.25 shows the typical view of how a river may develop these features.

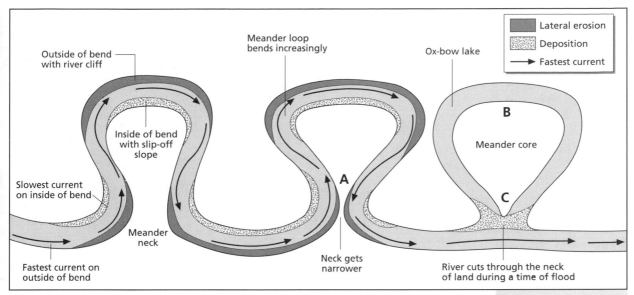

▲ Figure 1.25 How an ox-bow lake forms

At point A the faster currents on the outside of the two bends cause erosion and so the bends become closer, until they join. For a while the river flows around the old course at B and the new cut-off at C. Later on the old course will be sealed by material brought down in storms. The old bed will become a separate lake and eventually dry up and become fertile farmland. The name ox-bow may come from the shape of the lake being similar to the horns of an ox!

Causes and effects of river flooding

In autumn 1998 three English towns (Shrewsbury, Bewdley and Worcester) suffered flooding. One person died, cellars were flooded and hardship was caused, but the floods soon receded and life returned to normal. Insurance companies paid for most of the damage. In contrast, horrific flooding was caused by a hurricane in Nicaragua and Honduras (two LEDC examples). Here many rivers thundered through the landscape undermining hillslopes, causing landslides, washing away bridges, causing the deaths of *9000* people and generally wrecking the economy.

Flooding is most likely with rivers which:
- have steep valleys
- have impermeable soils such as clay, which does not let water infiltrate
- have plenty of streams
- are not used as a water supply
- have had the trees removed so that evapotranspiration is no longer possible
- run through built-up areas with tarmac covering the soil.

You will need to quote two case studies yourself. Learn the details of one flood in the UK, the EU, or an MEDC and one in an LEDC. If severe flooding has taken place since this guide or your textbook was published, collect details and learn all you can about it. Be sure you can write about the causes, effects and attempts to control future flooding in your example. *If you cannot, then learn a different example.*

Hints and Tips!

You will need to know an LEDC example **and** one from the UK or another MEDC.

Hints and Tips!

Instances of flooding are happening more often. Learn examples from the TV and newspapers but again make sure you have enough detail to answer the question – otherwise use examples from the textbooks.

Storm hydrographs

Draw Figure 1.26 several times to get the general features. What is happening in the diagram?

- It starts raining at 1400 hrs.
- By 1600 hrs the rain is at its heaviest.
- Between 1400 and 1800 hrs the rain is filling up the soil.
- Around 1700 hrs the soil is **saturated**, so the water moves directly to the river as **overland flow**.
- By 1800 hrs the river volume is increasing quite rapidly. The level is rising but the river will not actually flood unless it exceeds its bankful capacity.
- At some later time – hours, days or even weeks later – water moving through the soil and rock will reach the river.
- Notice that the volume drops at a different rate from the rate at which it rose.

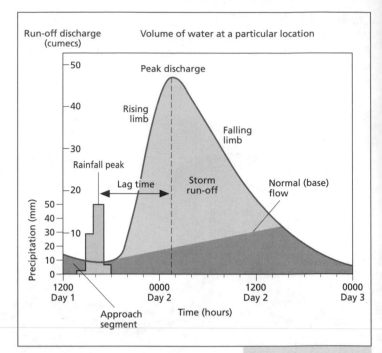

▲ Figure 1.26
A storm
hydrograph

Management of river flooding

There are a variety of ways to prepare for floods and these depend on the frequency of flooding, the nature of the landscape around the river, and the wealth of the country itself.

Know your case study

You will need to know in detail an example of the causes and effects of flooding and of flood management techniques in 1) the UK, the EU or an MEDC and 2) an LEDC. Study these two examples.

Events

	R Rhine Netherlands 31 January 1995	R Ganges and R Brahmaputra Bangladesh 1998
Natural causes Previous heavy rain	Prolonged heavy rain in December and January over much of Europe	Unusually heavy monsoon rain
	Ground saturated	Half of Bangladesh is just above the flood plain
Global warming (consequence of natural and human factors)	Rhine area now 40% more rain in last 100 years	12% of Bangladesh could easily disappear in the next 100 years
Human causes Changes upstream	Improved flood protection in Germany means more water goes straight down to the Netherlands	Ganges used for irrigation upstream. Less silt comes downstream to build up the floodplain

Case study *continued*

	R Rhine Netherlands 31 January 1995	R Ganges and R Brahmaputra Bangladesh 1998
Human causes Natural vegetation removed	Hedgerows removed. Less interception – rain goes straight to the river	Deforestation of trees in Nepal and Bhutan – less interception of rain
Urbanisation	Tarmac for roads and houses means less infiltration into the soil	Rising population means more wells, falling water table leads to slope collapse

Effects

Netherlands	Bangladesh
• Much farm land flooded • 4 people died • 250,000 people evacuated • 1 million cattle moved away	• Over half the country was flooded • 1040 people died • 23 million homeless • 130 million cattle drowned

Management of the situation

Management strategy	Netherlands	Bangladesh
Evacuation of people and livestock	✔	✔
Need for international cooperation	✔	✔
Afforestation upstream	✔	✔
Rebuilding of dykes	✔	✔
Early warning system	✔	✔
Creation of special areas of low quality land that can be deliberately flooded	✔	✔ Special shelters above flood level

See also the back of this book for a British example of severe flooding. The latest strategy is not to build concrete drainage which carries water rapidly to the rivers but to let the water flow slowly through gravel beds so the water arrives at the river over a long period of time and there is less actual flooding.

Examination Practice Questions

As you answer these questions notice any similarities to the two examples given above, then look at a suggested answer on page 112.

1 For a named example **in the UK** that you have studied, explain why a flood occurred.
What were the effects of the flood?
What was done afterwards to try and ensure the floods did not happen again? [7]

2 For a named example **in an LEDC** explain why floods occurred.
What were the effects of the floods?
What has been done to reduce the damage caused by further floods? [7]

Coasts

Key ideas
- Coastal erosion, transport and deposition processes produce distinct landscape features.
- What are the causes and effects of coastal erosion?
- How can coastal erosion be managed?

Key words and definitions

Attrition	pebbles in the water hit against each other and become smaller.
Backwash	water moving back down the beach.
Constructive waves	where the swash is greater than the backwash so beaches are built up.
Corrasion	pebbles in the water eroding the cliffs.
Corrosion	acids in the water dissolve rocks such as limestone.
Destructive waves	where the backwash is stronger than the swash. Beaches are slowly destroyed.
Groynes	barriers (usually wooden) built on the beach at right angles to the sea to trap stones and other sediment and so slow down longshore drift.
Hydraulic pressure	the sheer power of a wave which causes erosion.
Longshore drift	the movement of sediment along the coast by wave action.
Swash	water moving up the beach as an incoming wave.

Features and processes
Coasts are constantly being reshaped by powerful waves. In places erosion is predominant and in others deposition is the main process. The four erosion processes at work in the sea are the same as those found in rivers.

Hints and Tips!
Be able to describe the *processes* as much as the features they produce.

Headlands and bays
Look at Figure 1.27, which shows what happens when there is hard and soft rock in the same area.
- The soft rock is more rapidly worn away, forming bays.
- The hard rock is more resistant and so headlands are formed.
- As the headlands become more exposed so erosion from wind and waves becomes more intense.

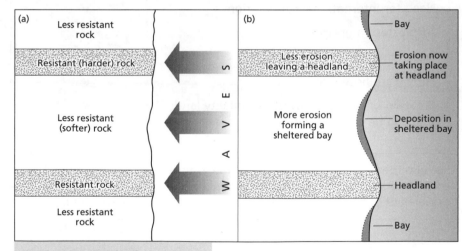

▲ Figure 1.27 The formation of headlands and bays

Cliffs
Wave cut notches are cut at the base of the cliff by the action of large waves at high tide. The notches get larger and eventually that section of the cliff collapses. This is repeated many times, so that the cliff edge 'retreats', leaving behind a platform that is exposed at low tide, as shown in Figure 1.28.

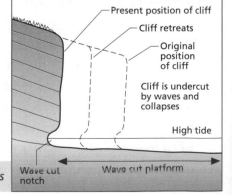

▶ Figure 1.28 Notches and platforms

Caves, arches and stacks

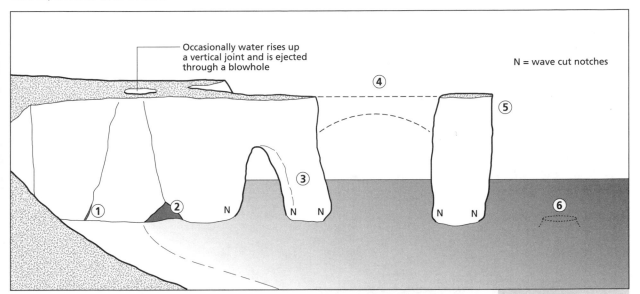

Occasionally water rises up
a vertical joint and is ejected
through a blowhole

N = wave cut notches

▲ Figure 1.29
Coastal features

Many cliffs are composed of hard rock, but cracks within the rock lead to a
series of inspiring coastal features, as shown in Figure 1.29. The general
sequence is straightforward and you should learn each stage in detail.
1. The sea finds and widens small cracks.
2. Cracks develop into small caves.
3. Caves extend, widen and deepen to form an arch. This process is speeded
   up if waves are attacking from the opposite side of the headland.
4. Continued undercutting leads to collapse of the arch, leaving a stack.
5. The stack is attacked at the base and collapses.
6. The remaining stump is eroded and finally disappears.

Hints and Tips!

An example of a
stack is Old Harry,
Dorset coast. An
example of an arch is
Durdle Door, also on
the Dorset coast.

Examination Practice Question

(a) Look at Figure 1.30. Which is the most resistant rock
    and why?   [2]

(b) Look at Figure 1.31. Describe the pattern of the rocks
    in relation to the sea. Describe how this coastline has
    changed over the years.   [5]

▶ Figure 1.30

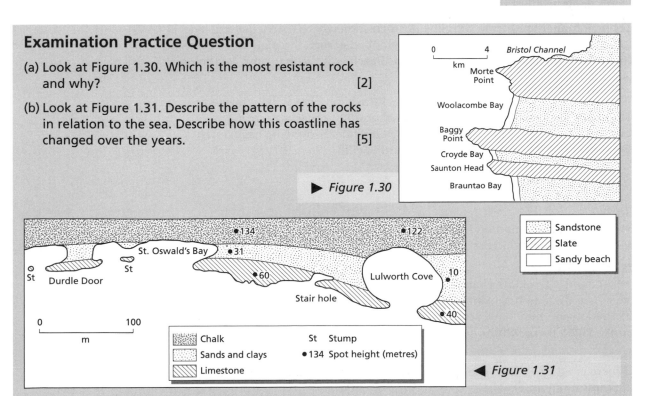

◀ Figure 1.31

Longshore drift: a process of erosion and deposition

Below are four technical words needed for your exam:
1. **Swash** – this is when the waves come up the beach
2. **Backwash** – when waves go back down the beach
3. **Constructive waves** – build up features as the swash is stronger than the backwash
4. **Destructive waves** – erode material owing to a powerful backwash.

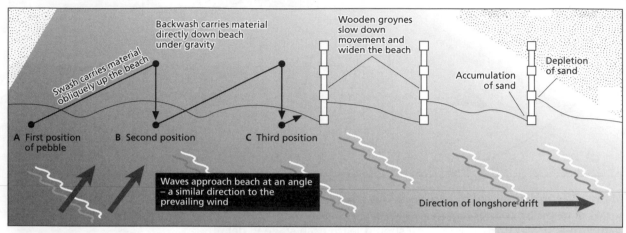

▲ Figure 1.32
Longshore drift

Figure 1.32 shows the movement of material along the coast by the waves, which is called longshore drift.

Influenced by the wind, the incoming waves (swash) carry material up the beach at an angle. As it loses its power the water drains straight down the beach under gravity. Later on another wave repeats the process so, for example, a grain of sand is carried in a zig-zag fashion along the beach. Don't imagine all of this happens in one day.

The material eroded from the cliffs must go somewhere. Carried along by longshore drift in the zig-zag fashion described earlier, the material is eventually deposited to form features such as **beaches**, **spits**, **bars** and **tombolos** (see below).

Where the swash is stronger than the backwash, beaches will be formed. The larger, heavier stones are carried further up the beach by strong incoming waves. The backwash can carry the finer sediments back down the beach, but the larger stones stay near the cliff.

Features of coastal deposition

Spits
Spits are made of sand and stones and extend out beyond the coastline, sometimes growing across river estuaries.

They usually occur:
- where the coastline changes
- where there is sufficient material to build the spit.

Examples you may have seen or studied are Dawlish Warren in Devon and Spurn Head in Yorkshire.

Bars
If there is no river, then the spit may reach right across the bay, for example at Shipton Bay in Devon.

Hints and Tips!

Have you been on a geography field trip? In the exam room don't forget to use what you saw and studied in the exam if it's relevant.

Tombolos

A tombolo is a spit which links an island to the mainland. Chesil Beach, which links the Dorset mainland to the island of Portland Bill at Weymouth, is a good example.

Look up www.getmapping.com on the Internet to find Portland Bill and Chesil Beach, then answer the following questions.
(a) Identify and follow the original coastline on the south west side of the picture.
(b) Identify the original island that existed off Portland.
(c) Find the point where Chesil Beach begins, then follow it all the way down to Portland Bill.

Questions

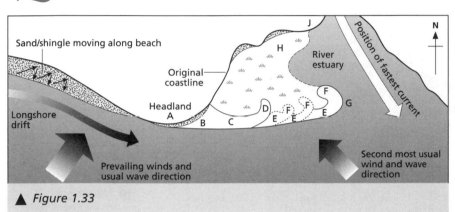

A-J original coastline
B-G the developing spit affected by different wind directions
H marshland developing behind the spit that will become solid ground in time

▲ *Figure 1.33*

Look at Figure 1.33. Consider and write down the effect of each of the following:

(a) Longshore drift

(b) The prevailing (most frequent) wind direction

(c) The second most usual wind and wave direction

(d) What stops the spit extending right across the river?

Note the steady build-up of marshland, which often creates a nature reserve and which later on becomes solid ground.

The causes, effects and management of coastal erosion

Coasts can be given protection from erosion by the following:
- Wooden fences called groynes, at right angles to the sea, slow down the waves and interrupt the flow of material along the beach. Material builds up on the side facing the wind.
- Breakwaters and piers are sometimes built to stabilise and build up a particular beach.
- Shingle (layers of rounded pebbles), whether occurring naturally or as a result of human interference, also protects the base of the cliff. Removal of that material can speed up coastal erosion.
- Revetments (sloping wooden barriers) are sometimes used as well as concrete sea walls.

Hints and Tips!

You will need a UK case study illustrating coastal erosion and its management.

Know your case study

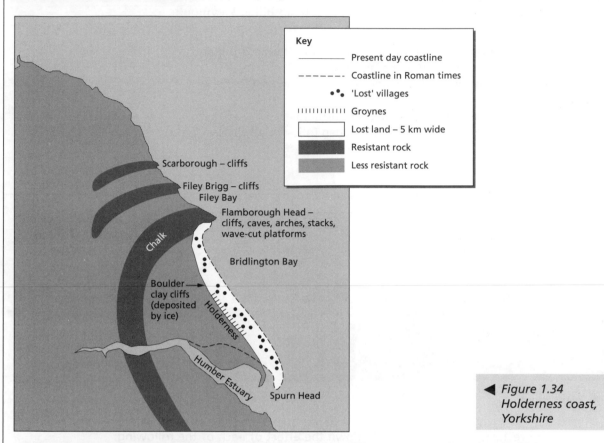

◀ Figure 1.34
Holderness coast,
Yorkshire

- The main rock is boulder clay (sand and clay) so the cliffs are very weak and unstable.
- The cliffs are retreating rapidly – over 1 metre a year.
- Towns 4 km from the sea in Roman times are now on the coast and under threat. Many villages, known about in the Middle Ages have long gone.

Do you think this coast should be protected or should nature be allowed to take its course?

Pause for thought for a few moments to answer this question. Give reasons for your answer.

Why should the coast be protected?

Hornsea (see the OS map in Figure 1.35) was judged to be a big enough town to justify expensive coastal protection (see groynes marked on Figure 1.35). Mappleton (22 44) is a relatively small village but the great cost of re-aligning the vital B1242 road, which virtually runs the length of the Holderness coast, meant the planners decided to protect that part of the coast instead of letting the sea do its worst.

Unfortunately, by protecting Mappleton the coast to the south has suffered greater erosion (10 metres a year) as a result. Sand that used to protect the cliffs is now blocked to the north of Mappleton.

A brave farmer, Sue Earl, kept her farm going at Great Cowden (23 42) despite losing fields year on year. In 1996 even the farm house went and she had to give up.

Notice how the coast cannot be protected for ever. The erosion is being managed, it is not being stopped. Protecting one area of coast often leads to pressure and even greater erosion on neighbouring stretches of coast.

Stop and Think

You may have seen the video of Sue's farm and the Mappleton defence scheme. Remember the problems shown there.

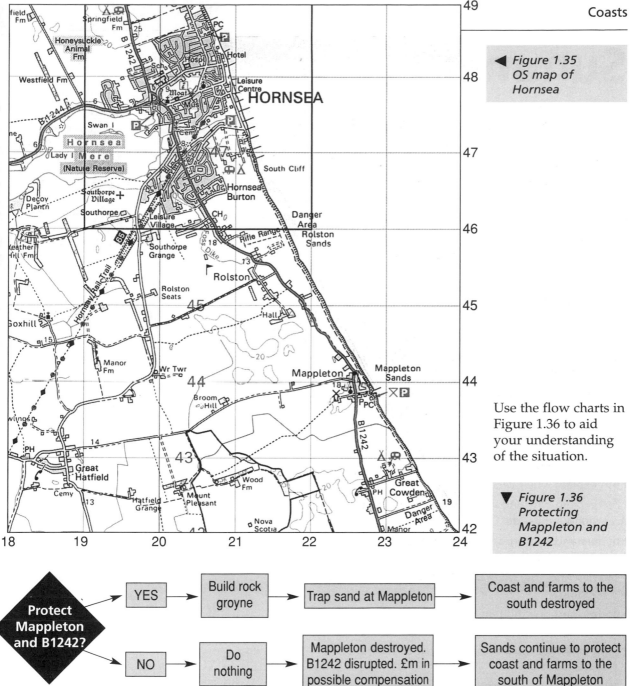

◀ *Figure 1.35 OS map of Hornsea*

Use the flow charts in Figure 1.36 to aid your understanding of the situation.

▼ *Figure 1.36 Protecting Mappleton and B1242*

Protect Mappleton and B1242?

YES → Build rock groyne → Trap sand at Mappleton → Coast and farms to the south destroyed

NO → Do nothing → Mappleton destroyed. B1242 disrupted. £m in possible compensation → Sands continue to protect coast and farms to the south of Mappleton

Take note that action at one location often has a knock on effect elsewhere. The planners must understand this as well as you.

Refer to your own notes for the questions below and then turn to the back for more named examples.

Examination Practice Question – higher level paper

(a) Name and describe a particular coastline which is experiencing significant erosion. Include its effect on the local population. [3]

(b) What attempts have there been to control the erosion? [2]

(c) How successful were those attempts? [2]

Hallsands in Devon, Barton in Dorset, and of course Holderness would be good examples.

Summary

Key words to know and understand

Attrition	Evapotranspiration	Meanders
Backwash	Groyne	Overland flow
Constructive waves	Hydraulic pressure	Plate margins
Corrosion	Infiltration	Saturation
Corrasion	Liquefaction	Subduction zone
Destructive waves	Longshore drift	Swash
Erosion	Magma	Transpiration

Hints and Tips!

Case studies are worth 7 marks out of 19 in a question. The exercise at the bottom is valuable in identifying the correct case studies, which in turn should help you to score high marks in the exam.

Check list for revision

	Understand and know	Needs more revision	Do not understand	Refer to pages
I understand why plate margins and volcanoes occur together.	☐	☐	☐	9
I understand why plate margins and earthquakes occur together.	☐	☐	☐	9
I understand and can name the main parts of the water cycle.	☐	☐	☐	18
I understand how waterfalls are formed.	☐	☐	☐	21
I can explain why rivers flood.	☐	☐	☐	21
I can explain why and where water travels fastest around a meander.	☐	☐	☐	22
I understand hydrographs and can explain why there is a lag time.	☐	☐	☐	24
I can describe how MEDCs and LEDCs try to 'manage' flooding.	☐	☐	☐	24
I understand how human activity can make flooding more likely.	☐	☐	☐	24
I can name and explain the processes of river and coastal erosion.	☐	☐	☐	26
I can describe how coastal features develop.	☐	☐	☐	28

Know your case studies

Which real places have you studied as an example of...

• a volcano	name:_____	p 13
• an earthquake	name:_____	p 11
• destructive (convergent) plates	name:_____	p 10
• divergent (constructive) plates	name:_____	p 9
• transform (conservative) plates	name:_____	p 10
• flooding in the United Kingdom, EU or MEDC	name:_____	p 24
• flooding in an LEDC	name:_____	p 23
• flood control	name:_____	pp 24, 25
• coastal erosion	name:_____	p 26
• coastal deposition	name:_____	p 28
• coastal management	name:_____	pp 29, 112

Unit 2: People and places to live

This unit covers the structure and distribution of populations, why populations rise and why people move. The second theme looks at the layout of cities in different countries, the problems caused by traffic and how to solve them, and again looks at the causes and consequences of people moving from place to place.

Population

Key ideas
- What factors affect the density and distribution of population between areas and within a country?
- How does population structure vary between countries?
- What are the causes and consequences of population growth?
- What are the causes and consequences of a recent international migration?

Candidates in the higher paper answer *one* of the two questions provided. Candidates in the foundation paper have only one question provided.

Key words and definitions

Birth rate	number of babies born per 1,000 people.
Death rate	number of deaths per 1,000 people.
Emigration	the movement of people out of a country.
Immigration	the movement of people into a country.
Migration	the movement of people from one area or country to another area or country.
Population control	attempts by a government to slow down the population increase in its country.
Population density	the number of people per square kilometre.
Population structure	the proportion of people in each age group. Also, the proportion of males to females.

Factors affecting the density and distribution of population
The density of population is the average number of people per square kilometre.

Compare:

	Japan	UK
Size	374,749 km²	241,590 km²
Population 1992	124,366,000	57,763,000
Population density	332 people per km²	239 people per km²

Therefore, Japan is a more crowded country.

Density, being an average, does hide population concentrations. In Japan, for example, few people live in the mountains – most live in the flat coastal area, making life even more crowded.

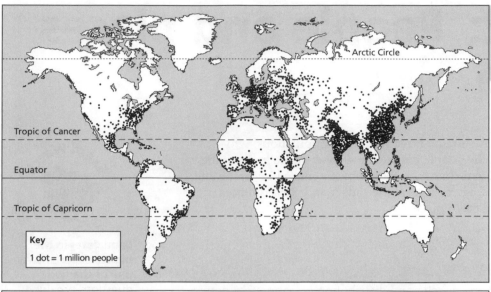

Figure 2.1 The most highly populated areas of the world

Key

1 dot = 1 million people

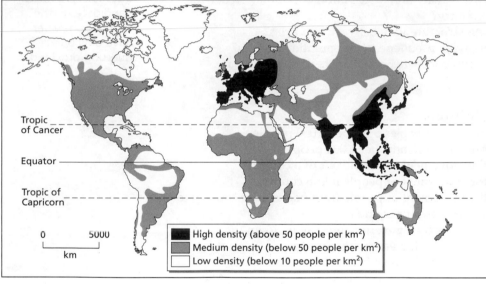

High density (above 50 people per km²)
Medium density (below 50 people per km²)
Low density (below 10 people per km²)

Figure 2.2 The most densely populated areas of the world

Test Yourself

Look at Figures 2.1 and 2.2, especially 2.1. Notice the variation. This is the very essence of world geography. Can you spot the crowded Nile Valley? Can you locate the empty Sahara?

Study the charts below.

Factors that cause low populations include:

Factor	Example	Reason
Mountains	Andes of South America	Steep-sided, difficult to farm, often cool temperatures, difficult to travel
Low rainfall	Sahara, North Africa	Difficult to grow crops/keep animals
Unreliable rainfall	Parts of Ethiopia	Monsoon rains, difficult to predict time of arrival each year
Low temperatures for much of the year	Siberia, Russia	Unpleasant, soil difficult to plough as ground is frozen for several months of the year
Vegetation – rainforests	Interior parts of Brazil	Difficult to move, create space or build anything on a large scale
Lack of economic potential	Andes of South America	No minerals, remote, poor transport. No reason for any economic activity to begin – lack of raw materials etc.

Factors that attract high populations include:

Factor	Example	Reason
Fertile river valleys	River Nile (Egypt)	Good farming over thousands of years
Fertile soils near volcanoes	Island of Montserrat (West Indies)	Ash from volcanoes is fertile and leads to good farming
Large areas of flat land	River Brahmaputra (Bangladesh)	80% of Bangladesh is about 5 metres above sea level
Climate – reliable rainfall	Britain	Crops will grow year after year as Britain has a steady and reliable rainfall pattern
Climate – high temperatures and sunshine	California, western USA	Crops ripen easily, e.g. oranges. Attracts film-makers and related leisure industries. Most people enjoy the sunshine
Regular water supply	Western Europe	In the time before taps and pumped water everyone lived near rivers and springs. Guaranteed harvests attract people and lead to settlements
Economic prosperity	Northwest Europe, California and Japan	As many countries move away from farming as a source of employment, economic prosperity needs good transport and shopping links. This is called the infrastructure

Questions

It is important to know the main factors and to link them clearly and precisely to a specific area.

Photocopy Figures 2.1 and 2.2 and enlarge them if possible. Go through each reason for high populations mentioned above and write them on Figure 2.1. Then go through the reasons for low populations, marking them on Figure 2.2. Add appropriate titles. This will be a useful atlas exercise, building up your locational knowledge and serving as a means of revising the above information. As the atlas provides your information the answers to this question are not found in the guide.

Variations in population density between areas of a country

People are not evenly spread across a country. Look at the differences in population density and where all main towns are. Be ready to explain the variations. These might be because of:
- relief – where mountains and flat land are found
- economic reasons – perhaps raw materials were/are found in the area, giving rise to particular industries
- historical reasons – the region might include areas that were once of historical importance, perhaps in controlling that area (castles, Roman forts etc.)
- climate – highland areas tend to be cold and wet. This deters most people, but the wet ground might give rise to certain types of farming.

You do not need your own case study but be prepared to analyse one given in the exam. Study page 36 as an example.

Hints and Tips!

Never say 'good climate'. What is good for an Inuit is not good for a Saharan herder. Also, it is imprecise, and you must give clear, detailed answers in all your exams.

South Wales – an example of varying population densities

Much of South Wales is a mountainous region with hills above 500 metres. Along the southern strip of the region is flatter, lower land. Cutting through the mountains are valleys running north to south, which are exploited by rail and road routes.

Although beautiful, the mountains themselves are cold and steep-sided and deter most people. The people who do live there tend to be connected with sheep farming. The mountains and valleys of South Wales were once major world centres for coal mining and the related iron and steel industries. The raw materials were found in the valleys, so that is where the industries developed and where the people came to live.

Today the raw materials are mainly used up and much of the industry has moved into the southern strip of the region. However, the former mining and steel towns, such as Merthyr Tydfil, Ebbw Vale and Tredegar, still survive, although attracting new employment is proving difficult.

The most southerly strip, including the M4 running east to west, and the ports of Cardiff, Swansea and Port Talbot, has attracted modern manufacturing industry such as the Royal Mint and Ford's engine plant at Bridgend as well as tertiary activities such as the Driver and Vehicle Licence Centre at Swansea. All these activities attract people in great numbers to live in this southern strip.

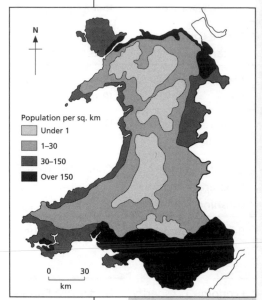

N

Population per sq. km
- Under 1
- 1–30
- 30–150
- Over 150

0   30
km

▲ Figure 2.3 Population in Wales

Variations in population structure between countries

The population structure shows the proportion of the different age groups in a population. In wealthy countries, old people are looked after and financially supported (through pensions and medical care) by the younger working population. The latter also looks after and pays for children and young people, providing care, education and medical assistance. The percentage of children and old people in relation to the working population is therefore very important. This is also true of LEDCs, although the financial responsibilities are not as great.

Study Figure 2.4, which is divided into male and female and into age groups at 5-year intervals. Notice how the male/female balance is about equal up to 35 years of age, after which there is a greater proportion of females in each age group – showing that women live longer than men do. Notice also the greater percentage of very young children. This is because many babies are born, but many die young (high birth and death rates).

In contrast, Figure 2.5 shows the structure for a more economically developed country such as Britain. Again, females live longer than males but notice the low percentage of young children, indicating a low birth rate and a low death rate. *Almost* everyone born in the UK lives to at least 60. No one lives forever of course, and so the 60+ age groups become progressively smaller.

Remember, the starting age for work varies from country to country. In the UK it is 16, but in countries with no free secondary education it could be 12

Test Yourself

List the reasons why there is a great variation in population density. Include what you learned on the previous page.

or even lower. In the UK the official retirement age is moving towards 65. In many less economically developed countries there is no pension, so farmers and their families never 'retire'. They struggle on as best they can until their strength gives out.

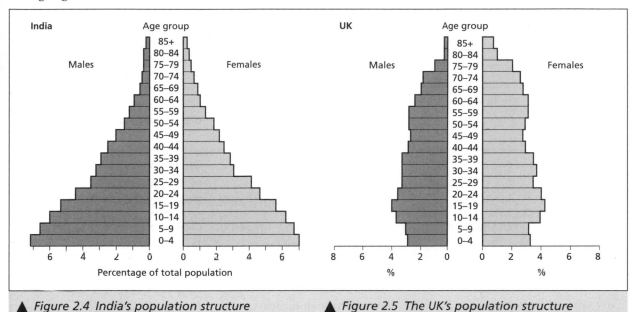

▲ Figure 2.4 India's population structure   ▲ Figure 2.5 The UK's population structure

`People of official working age provide the money for everyone else, either as individuals or as taxpayers. A relatively small working group having to care for a *large group* of dependants creates economic pressures on those working individuals. In many less developed countries such as India most dependants are young children; in the UK most are old people. In the UK in 1998 the dependency ratio was 62·75. This means that for every 100 people of working age (between 16 and 60/64) there were 62·75 people dependent on them (children 0–16 and the elderly – women over 60 and men over 65).

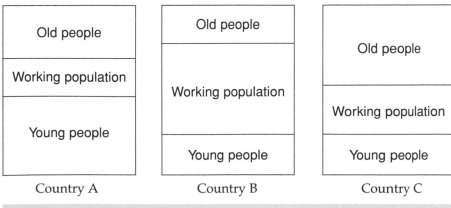

▲ Figure 2.6 Working population and dependants

Since the mid-1960s the number of births in the UK has fallen dramatically (see Figure 2.5). People are now living a lot longer, putting pressure on the government's finances.

In country A, the working population has to support a very large percentage of dependent young people. Taxes will be high or benefits will be low.

In country B the percentage of dependants is low. Taxes will be low even if the benefits to both young and old dependants are high.

What will be the situation in country C?

Age group	Needs	What is provided and by whom	
		MEDC country, e.g. UK	LEDC country, e.g. Kenya
Young people	Food/clothing	By parents	By parents
	Education	Free education for all up to 18	Parents pay, so some children, mainly boys, receive primary education. Very few receive secondary education
	Medical care	Free treatment paid for by the taxpayer through the government	Only very basic medical care – often just a nurse or a clinic
Old people	Food	Pensions (paid by the taxpayers in the economically working group)	Old people carry on farming or receive support from children. No state help
	Housing and heating	Residential homes – funded by individuals and the government	Looked after by the family as far as possible
	Medical care	'Free' treatment, wheelchairs, hip replacements, heart operations, care by social services – meals on wheels	Only basic care from their family

Questions

In the UK in 1995 the retirement age for women was 60 and for men was 65. The government has decided that the retirement age will be slowly raised to 65 for everyone.

(a) Will the dependency ratio rise or fall? Give reasons.

(b) Why did the government raise the age to 65 for all and not go for a retirement age of 61/62 years for all?

Hints and Tips!
Make a copy of this summary. Have a look at it once a day for 5 minutes and try to learn one bit at a time.

The causes and consequences of population growth
Most countries have experienced population growth. Some developed countries e.g. the UK are now seeing a slowing down of the rate of increase, and soon some countries may find their population has levelled off or is actually falling. Japan's population may even halve in your lifetime.

Make sure you understand the following:
- Birth rate – the number of births for every 1,000 people in the population
- Death rate – the number of deaths per 1,000 people
- The natural increase is the birth rate with the death rate taken away.

A *large* natural increase takes place when birth rates are high and death rates are low. Several factors affect this:

Birth rate high	• No birth control or sex education (because of lack of money or religious beliefs) • Parents have many children knowing some will die • Several children are needed to support the family, especially in the parents' old age
Death rate low	• Simple medical care is available to keep sick children alive • Water supplies are improved, reducing the risk of water-borne killer diseases such as cholera

A *small* natural increase occurs when birth rates *and* death rates are high, or when both are low.

In Britain where both birth and death rates are low, this happened for several reasons, including:
- The contraceptive pill has been available since 1963
- The law has allowed abortion since 1968
- Most children survive, so there is no need to have children as an 'insurance' against some dying young
- More sex education in schools so fewer children are conceived
- Couples marry later
- Rapid developments in health care e.g. heart bypass operations, new drugs, greater understanding of the human body
- Better diet
- Fewer major military conflicts involving UK people
- Women choose careers rather than have families, or start families later and so have fewer children in total.

Having too many people puts a strain on:
- Food supplies
- Raw materials
- Available jobs
- Available (and unchangeable) land supplies.

Hints and Tips!

Try to understand and remember all these reasons. A few countries are now worrying about not having enough people to keep their economies going. Most attempts at population management have been to reduce growth.

Hints and Tips!

You need one case study illustrating strategies to influence population change

Know your case study

Population control

China's policy
Some countries have felt the need to try and control their population numbers. China and India are well-known examples.

1950s	Large families encouraged in order to make China a strong nation
1960s	The population grew rapidly without the government's encouragement
1970s	Advertising and family planning policies tried but population continued to rise, threatening to double in size in only 50 years
1980s	'One child policy'. Incentives included free education, better housing etc. Large fines imposed and incentives lost if other children born. Couples had to get state approval to get married. Enforced abortions and sterilisation became the policy
1990s	Public protests force change of policy. Second child is allowed in rural areas (difficult to control people in remote areas). Also in rural areas if first child is a girl a second child may be permitted

Case study *continued*

Effects of this policy
The birth rate fell from 40 per 1000 in 1968 to 17 per 1000 in 1980. The family size has fallen from 5.8 to 2.4 in 20 years. However, China's population has already passed 1200 million people. It is estimated that this policy has curbed population growth by 300 million in 20 years.

Reactions to the policy
Remember, China is a Communist country and its people are used to the government controlling aspects of their lives we in Britain would consider to be personal matters. A government supporter would see the value to China of limiting the population increase and would accept the personal limitations. Others would (and did) resent being told when to marry and how many children to have. Enforced abortions and sterilisations are an abuse of very personal freedoms to British people. Whatever your attitude, in China boys are valued more than girls as they are seen to be of more use in the fields. Be objective in your answers. Report the facts on Chinese perceptions as they are without bringing in your own personal view. Recent reports show a shortage of girls – warning of the dangers of population manipulation.

Hints and Tips!
Do not confuse China with Japan. Japan has no population control policy.

Several countries, such as China, India and Sri Lanka, have tried fairly dramatic schemes to force couples to have fewer children. The UK policy has been one of education, free/cheap birth control, and women choosing careers rather than large families.

Hints and Tips!
List the arguments for and against population control. Be objective.

Questions

From your school notes write about the population control policy of one country. Explain the policy, the reasons for it, and people's reaction to it. Compare your notes with the case study above.

The causes and consequences of a recent international migration

So far we have looked at changes to a country's own people. Immigration – the moving into a country of other people – and emigration, where people leave a country and go elsewhere – will also affect a country's total population. International migration means moving from one country to another.

In this section you need to understand *why* people leave their home country – a place they probably know, love, and would normally feel secure in – what drives them out and what attracts them to somewhere else. Understand too what the effects of migration are on the country that loses its most active people, on the country that receives them, and on the migrants themselves. One case study is sufficient but **necessary** for this section.

Know your case study

Turks to Germany

Learn the following true account and try to visualise the pictures in your mind to help you remember. Note that other countries also receive workers from elsewhere, and they too suffer similar problems. An alternative named example is Mexicans moving into the USA.

1960 Turkey. Much unemployment and low wages.

Germany. Shortage of workers in factories to do unskilled jobs.

Turkish workers welcomed with open arms – called 'guest workers'.

Turkish men encouraged their wives and children to come. They went to the cheapest areas. They found it difficult to learn German. The two groups became isolated from each other.

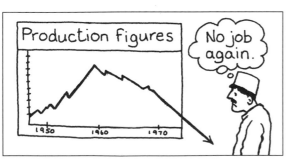

1970s – hard economic times. Many factories close. German unemployment around 10%. Turks in Germany suffered around 20% unemployment.

Resentment and suspicion between the two groups. Turks stay in Germany despite conditions. Germany still needed its guest workers to work in hospitals and do the lowest-paid jobs.

Questions

(a) Why do the Turks not go back to Turkey? Think back to Picture 1.

(b) What would happen to Germany if all the Turks did go back?

(c) What is the effect on Turkey of having many of its dynamic people elsewhere?

Hints and Tips!

Try to memorise the pictures and then recall them in the exam if relevant to the question.

Settlement

Key ideas

- People migrate (move) from rural areas to urban areas in the hope of a better life. This is not always achieved.
- City authorities in LEDCs cannot cope so assisted self-help is often the main approach to progress.
- Cities have different zones, each with its own characteristics.
- The impact of traffic in an urban area and strategies to manage that.
- Cities and towns depend on each other for a variety of goods and services.
- Causes and consequences of urban to rural migration.

Key words and definitions

Central business district	the business part of a town centre characterised by office blocks, hotels and large expensive shops.
Green belts	area of protected countryside around a city. No one may build in these areas without special permission.
Integrated transport system	where bus and train services are linked or coordinated. Bus stops may be situated outside the rail stations. Special tickets may cover bus and train journeys.
Retail park	a collection of modern shops on the edge of town near a motorway junction or main road to allow good accessibility.
Rural	countryside.
Settlement	a city, town or village. Anywhere that people live.
Settlement hierarchy	the idea that in any given area there will be one or two large cities, more towns and many villages.
Shanty towns	poor and unplanned settlements on the edge of planned wealthy cities.
Sphere of influence	an area where customers are attracted to a particular shop or town.
Suburbs	areas of a city often a few miles from the town centre.
Threshold population	the smallest number of people needed in an area to make a shop profitable.
Urban	towns and cities.

The causes of rural to urban migration

In poorer parts of the world people are moving from the countryside to the town. It is important to understand that not all countryside is as attractive as it is in Britain: in some parts of the world it is very hard and depressing.

The reasons people leave the countryside are called **push factors**. Use PUSHED to help you to remember:

- **P**ressure on land so many have to leave
- **U**nemployment in the countryside
- **S**anitation – poor/non-existent in the countryside. Often no running water or clinics
- **H**ardship – often a harsh climate
- **E**ducation – very little, if any
- **D**isasters – drought, famine, civil war etc.

The reasons why people are attracted to the cities are called **pull factors**, e.g.

- Better-paid jobs
- Factory jobs which are not dependent on the weather
- Education for their children
- Health-care facilities (clinics and hospitals)
- The general belief that life is better there (the 'bright lights' effect).

Hints and Tips!

You need one case study to illustrate push and pull factors, effects on rural areas and shanty town development. Examples might include India or Brazil.

Consequences of rural to urban migration

It is important to realise straight away that the layout of cities in poorer countries is different from cities in Britain. You will know by now that in the UK good transport enabled richer people to move away from town centres, so that the wealthier people are on the edge of town, the poorer people near the centre. In less developed countries it is *the complete opposite*, and you mustn't get confused. Poor transport in LEDC countries means that the rich stay near the centre. They have been there a long time. So many people have flocked to the cities that there is no space in the town for any newcomers, and also the city authorities are overwhelmed. Calcutta, in India, receives *300 new families a day*. So, anyone arriving from the countryside has to find a space – literally a small piece of ground on the edge of town – and build their own shelter.

These unplanned developments are called **bustees** in India (**favelas** in Brazil and **shanties** in Africa). People actually choose to live on or near rubbish tips as these provide the raw materials for their houses. Others live on hillsides or near swamps – anywhere that nobody else wants. There are many common features in these shanty towns:

- Poor housing – small shacks, self-built, no running water or legal power supply or systems to deal with sewage.
- Poor health due to overcrowding, contaminated water and lack of enclosed sewerage systems.
- Difficult to keep families together. Lack of contraception means large families.
- Lack of parental control can lead to crime in the main city.
- Families have to create jobs or travel long distances each day into the main city to obtain low-skill, low-paid jobs.

In peacetime it is usually the brightest people and those with initiative that tend to move for better opportunities. This means that the rural areas can be robbed of the very people who might have improved those areas. Change is very slow in such circumstances. Farming practices remain unchanged, while education and medical resources can be slow in coming as the

Stop and Think

Remember, life in the countryside can be much worse even than in the shanty towns.

Know your case study

Improving the quality of life in squatter settlements

Imagine being the housing officer in São Paulo (Brazil) or Calcutta (India). You live in a poor city in a poor country, and yet you have to house 300 extra families a day! Obviously an impossible task. What are your options?

1. Use the army to clear away the unsightly huts. South Africa briefly tried this in the past and soon gave up. The people ran away for a day, then came back and quickly rebuilt their huts.
2. Provide the materials for the newcomers, plan the layout of the settlement, provide basic water and sewerage, but let the people build their own homes. This allows for a

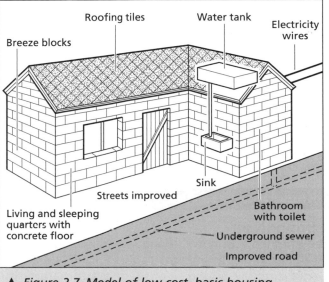

▲ *Figure 2.7 Model of low-cost, basic housing*

Labels: Roofing tiles · Water tank · Electricity wires · Breeze blocks · Sink · Streets improved · Living and sleeping quarters with concrete floor · Bathroom with toilet · Underground sewer · Improved road

Case study *continued*

sense of ownership and pride, as well as hope. It also keeps down the cost to the city. São Paulo uses this method.

3. Provide low-cost 'basic' houses. Several schemes have been tried – one used breezeblocks (cheap and easy to use) as the material for the main walls (see Figure 2.7). São Paulo tries this approach.
4. Unfortunately, the more the shanty towns are improved the more people will come to them. The real solution is to tackle the underlying cause of the original migration. If the rural areas had schools, hospitals, employment, clean water etc. there would be less need to move to the cities. To provide all these facilities in all villages would clearly be far too expensive but Bangladesh is developing this policy under its 'back to home' project.
5. Some countries are building new towns (e.g. Brasilia in Brazil and Sadat City, Egypt), with the main aim of taking pressure off the existing cities.

innovators have left for the cities. People often remain poor, badly fed and without any real skills in these circumstances.

The characteristics of land use zones in cities in wealthy countries

Study a city and you will notice certain areas have the same characteristics. An American called Burgess simplified it all into the diagram in Figure 2.8.

This zoning happens because:
1. Wealthier people steadily move towards the countryside and the less wealthy follow them.
2. Land is very expensive in the city centre, and so the cheapest land is on the edge of town. People with large houses favour areas where the land is cheaper.

You **must** be able to quote details of a case study to show the characteristics of the CBD, inner zones, outer suburbs and the rural/urban fringe of a British city. Take time to think about your local area. Take note of any fieldwork you have done.

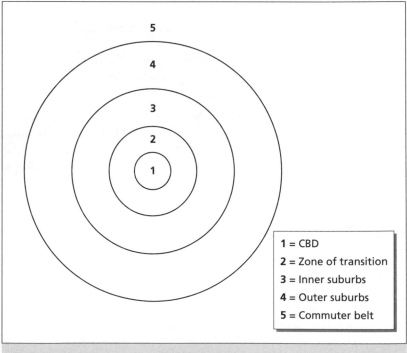

1 = CBD
2 = Zone of transition
3 = Inner suburbs
4 = Outer suburbs
5 = Commuter belt

▲ *Figure 2.8 Burgess' model of land use*

Study the example given below and compare it with your area or other published examples such as Swansea. What are the common characteristics?

Know your case study

Birmingham

Birmingham is Britain's second-largest city, so it is not surprising that all of the examples of land use can be found here. Read the following pages carefully, noting all of the relevant characteristics. Either identify your own examples or learn the ones given here.

Hints and Tips!

Review your notes comparing the structure of towns in MEDCs and LEDCs. They are different.

Central Business District (CBD)

This is an American term that you need to learn and refers to the specialist business area. In Birmingham, the CBD includes the Bull Ring shopping centre, New Street, Corporation Street, Smallbrook Ringway, and the new business area in Broad Street including the Hyatt Hotel and the National Indoor Area. The typical characteristics of a CBD include large shops (for example, Rackhams), large office blocks (NatWest Bank and the famous Rotunda), car showrooms such as Bristol Street Motors, a main railway station, a cathedral or large church, and a town hall. All CBDs share these common factors:

- Built on the most expensive land – that is where the customers are.
- Contain the tallest buildings (that is, buildings that maximise their use of vertical space) – because land is expensive.
- Have a much larger sphere of influence compared with small shopping centres in the suburbs. People come to work and shop in Birmingham from Worcester in the southwest and from Tamworth and beyond in the northeast.
- No longer contain houses – again, because the land is too expensive.
- Often have an inner ring road around them.

Inner Zones

Beyond the warehouse zone, which surrounds the CBD, are the inner zones that have not yet been redeveloped. In Birmingham, such areas include Sparkbrook, Sparkhill and Saltley. These areas were built to house workers from the railway, factories and other industries. These houses are now more than 100 years old. Typical characteristics include:
- grid pattern of roads (made up of long, straight roads joining others at 90°)
- terraced housing
- small front gardens, or no gardens at all, and small backyards
- no garages, so on-street parking, car theft and damage is a problem
- many houses have small rooms – usually two downstairs and two upstairs rooms. This leads to high-density housing where many small houses are squeezed into a given area.
- there are often factories in these areas, providing employment near to people's homes. In the past, they have caused a lot of air pollution but many such as the battery factory in Selly Oak and the Bird's custard factory in Digbeth have now been closed. The companies have moved to more spacious industrial estates nearer the motorways on the edge of the city.

Hints and Tips!

Think of an urban area near you that fits this description. Try to picture it in your mind. Also think of TV programmes such as EastEnders. Do not write about the characters in the exam room though!

Hints and Tips!

As you travel around, look out for different housing zones. Look at their characteristics and try to memorise them in writing or picture form ready for the exam.

At one time many houses were rented from the council or other landowners. From the 1980s onwards people were encouraged to buy their own houses, and the percentage of owner-occupied houses in this sector has risen sharply.

Questions

Look at Figure 2.9. What other problems are there of living in inner-city areas?

◀ *Figure 2.9 Typical view of inner city zone*

Advantages:
- Relatively cheap to buy houses. For example, in 1999 it cost £30,000 to buy a house in Sparkbrook, compared to £60,000 in Selly Oak, further away from the centre.
- Near the town centre, so travel to shops and work is quick, cheap and convenient – a bus ride of about 10 minutes.
- Often a sense of community, as people meet each other frequently.
- Sometimes there will be a local park, but otherwise very little evidence of trees, plants, grass etc.

Who lives there?
Mainly people on low incomes, immigrants from other countries seeking to improve their standard of living, students who rent property while at university, those who are unemployed for long periods of time, people who have few skills and therefore cannot get the higher-paid jobs to afford the houses in the suburbs. Sometimes wealthy outsiders buy property to improve it and then sell it for a higher price.

What is being done to improve these areas?
Since 1945 local councils have followed a combination of three strategies:
1. Knock down all the houses and build flats
2. Knock down all the houses and move people to the edge of the city where there is space
3. Refurbish the old houses so they will last another 50–100 years.

Flats
Whether in the redeveloped area or on the edge of town, blocks of flats have led to problems such as:
- uprooted communities
- lack of identity and belonging
- crime and vandalism
- conflict between neighbours
- lack of facilities for children and young people.

Many tower blocks that were built in the 1950s and 1960s have now been demolished, for example in the Bartley Green area of Birmingham.

The suburbs
These areas are very different in appearance to the inner zones. Edgbaston in southwest Birmingham, for example, is a very leafy suburb. Like many suburbs it has:
- semi detached and large detached houses
- front and back gardens
- houses with at least one garage
- a more relaxed street design – often with quiet traffic-free cul-de-sacs
- the countryside is close at hand – the Lickey Hills can be reached in 15 minutes or less
- no industry is allowed in the area.

The disadvantages of living in a suburb are that:
- it takes longer to reach the city centre shops and offices – a typical journey can take 20 minutes or more in the rush hour.
- the houses are very expensive – many cost more than £100,000.
- there is less sense of a community than in inner zones, because the houses are large, people are wealthy enough to be independent and they travel by car, so they rarely meet their neighbours.

Stop and Think

People often say the sense of community is less in urban areas because people meet less often. What do you think?

Did you know that in 1991 there were still 1,000,000 people in Britain who did not have hot water, or an inside toilet?

Hints and Tips!

You will need to know in detail a case study of urban regeneration AND a case study of traffic management in towns.

Who lives there?

People on high incomes who can afford items such as central heating or more than one car, and who are able to buy their own homes. This group has less unemployment, but no group is totally free from this threat.

Green belts

These are areas of countryside around the major cities which are now protected by law from further development. This is to give townspeople access to the countryside as well as protecting some of our best rural areas. Obviously roads and railways pass through the green belt, but new building must take place in the city or beyond the designated green belt land. Sometimes development does happen in green belt areas, but only in special cases and often after public outcry. Find out if your town has protected green belt countryside around it.

Strategies to improve the quality of life in urban areas

Part 1: Housing

It took the planners a long time to realise it but now most people appreciate that just putting up a few buildings does not create a community. Housing districts eventually get old and worn and need revitalising from time to time.

What examples are there of town councils trying to improve people's quality of life in urban Britain?

1. **Glasgow's GEAR project** – which tried to tackle great overcrowding in small very old slums by putting everyone into tower blocks. The buildings proved inadequate but, more seriously, the sense of community broke down for reasons mentioned earlier (see page 46). A change of policy meant more houses and fewer people in flats and it became a successful project.

2. **London's Dockland** – here old derelict docklands were replaced by expensive office blocks and very expensive accommodation.

3. **Townshill suburb, Swansea** – here the challenge was not so much the houses but the loss of hope in the future, not so much a need for bricks but for building a community. So:
   - depressing areas were grassed over by the local people
   - roads were made safe for all users
   - mind-sapping, long-term unemployment was tackled by setting up training courses.

The hope is that these and other measures will give a stability to this community, bring employment and give a purpose to life, turning it into a 'can do' community.

Other projects involve the relocation of factories away from housing areas. Whatever example you use, remember the theme is planning to improve the quality of life of the residents.

Hints and Tips!

Which type of zone do you live in? Don't be afraid to write about your area if it fits the question. Do not ramble on about minor points but use this book as a guide to what is expected.

Hints and Tips!

What was your coursework on? Be prepared to use the details in that coursework if it fits the question.

Hints and Tips!

You need one case study illustrating urban regeneration. A sample answer appears on page 114.

Part 2: Managing traffic in urban areas

Most towns existed long before cars were invented. Their layout therefore often involves narrow streets, small shops and narrow entrances to loading bays. Now that most people travel by car, and goods are delivered to shops by large lorries, towns and cities are clogged up by traffic.

For a long time planners have been trying to reduce the effects of traffic while attempting to preserve the character of our towns.

Problem: Too much traffic in towns not designed for cars and lorries.

Strategy 1. Restrict traffic – do all you can to reduce the traffic in towns – build by-passes, pedestrianise streets etc.

Strategy 2. Make public transport (trains, buses, modern trams) more attractive so people will want to leave their cars at home.

Most town planners have plans that use both Strategy 1 and Strategy 2.

Strategy 1: Restrict traffic in towns
Various ideas:
- By-passes and ring roads taking long-distance traffic around the town.
- Restricting parking and unloading in town centres.
- Banning traffic from some streets and paving them over so only pedestrians can use them.
- Banning heavy lorries on certain town centre roads.
- Making city centre car parking extremely expensive.

> ### Hints and Tips!
> You will need to know the details of one scheme in a more advanced country which tries to tackle this problem.

◀ *Figure 2.10 Slowing down and restricting traffic*

These restrictive policies are often linked to attempts to persuade people to travel by public transport, thereby reducing traffic congestion. This will only work if people see public transport as being better than the car.

Test Yourself
Look at the map of Beverley on page 107. Find the A1079(T) by-passing the town. Think how much time this by-pass saves the motorists compared with going through the town.

Strategy 2: Making public transport more attractive

Buses and local trains are less convenient than the car but passengers do not have the problem of parking. Also, not everyone owns a car.

An integrated public transport system is one where:
- local train and bus services are planned together, e.g. buses call at local stations to make connections easier.
- sometimes buses are timed to leave stations shortly after local trains arrive, etc.
- season tickets are available that cover local trains and buses.
- one local organisation is responsible for all public transport in the area, so that resources are used in the best possible way.
- large car parks are built at local stations to reduce in-town traffic.
- bus lanes are created to speed buses through the busy traffic in the rush hours.

Buses are space efficient: they carry about 60 passengers in the space taken up by four cars. However, despite bus lanes they can be slow. Local trains are fast but stop at only a few places.

Several big cities such as Manchester and Sheffield have now developed modern tram systems which combine the benefits of these two methods of transport.

In addition, cities such as Glasgow and Cambridge encourage cycling by providing cycles lanes, cycle lockers at local stations and free carriage of cycles on local trains.

▲ *Figure 2.11 New metro system running between Birmingham and Wolverhampton*

Provision of services in urban and rural areas

In geography the word 'services' means jobs such as hairdressing, financial advice, education etc. People in this sector do not make things but they help the primary and secondary industries to flourish.

There are two main categories of products we buy:
1. **High-order goods and services**
   - expensive (e.g. new car, television, legal advice)
   - bought less frequently
   - people are prepared to travel a long way to get them.
2. **Low-order goods and services**
   - cheap (e.g. crisps, newspapers etc.)
   - bought almost daily
   - people will only travel a short distance to buy them.

It therefore follows that a shop selling a product which is bought every day only needs a few hundred *local* customers in order to make a profit. The minimum number of *possible* customers is called the **threshold population**. Below this number the shop will make a loss.

Shops that sell high-order goods obviously need a greater number of possible customers because they make purchases less frequently. Marks and Spencer needs 50,000 people in an area before their store can make a profit.

Villages, towns and cities also have threshold populations. A large city centre selling high-order goods needs a large population to survive. A village selling low-order goods needs only a few hundred shoppers to survive. This being the case, in a large region there will be only one or two cities, several towns and many villages. This can be shown in a diagram (see Figure 2.12). This arrangement is called a **hierarchy**, with one city at the top and several villages at the base.

The area a shop, village or city serves is called its **sphere of influence**. A village shop only serves a small area, whereas a large city like London has a huge sphere of influence.

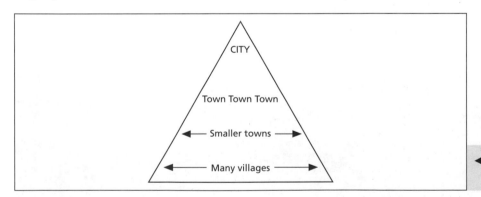

Figure 2.12 Settlement hierachy

How do geographers work out the sphere of influence of a settlement?
1. Ask shoppers in the street where they live.
2. Ask shopkeepers where their customers live.
3. They may visit people at home and ask where they shop.

The results are then mapped to show the sphere of influence.

!

Stop and Think

Your school has a *hierarchy* of authority. Draw a diagram showing the head teacher at the top, heads of department, classroom teachers and pupils at the bottom.

Check that you understand this flow chart of ideas:

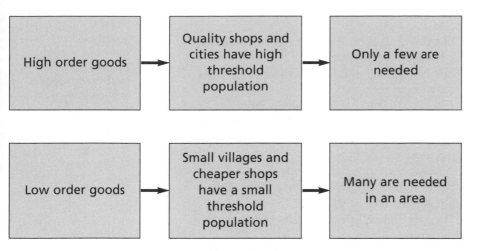

Neighbourhood shopping centres

These are designed to cater for the everyday needs of a local community, e.g. at Offmore in Kidderminster. Obviously they will supply low-order goods, e.g. newspapers and sweets, as well as services such as hairdressers. The centre will be small and people will not travel far to get there.

Does your area have a neighbourhood shopping centre? If so, list all the shops and what they provide. If not, then list five shops you would use on a regular basis.

Out-of-town shopping centres

These centres have developed in the last twenty years as town centres have become congested and more people have cars. Shoppers like them but planners and owners of shops in the town centre have their doubts.

Most of these out-of-town centres contain a large but predictable selection of shops, most of which appear in any shopping centre. They contain very few small family or specialist shops.

Although popular with shoppers, many people oppose such centres and the government has now banned any new developments not already approved.

Problems caused by out-of-town centres
- Traffic congestion around the centres
- Customers lured from the town centres
- Quality shops moving to the out-of-town centre
- Empty shops or low-quality shops in the old town centre
- Difficulty in attracting new quality shops
- Death of the old town centre?

Meadowhall, Sheffield

Meadowhall is a large shopping centre built on the outskirts of Sheffield. Like many out-of-town centres it has a number of characteristics. These can be remembered using CAR SPACES to help you:

C	Cheap land	Meadowhall is built on the edge of Sheffield where land is cheaper.
A	Accessible	The nearby M1 and local A roads mean it is easy to get to.
R	Redeveloped land	The site used to be an old steelworks.
S	Sphere of influence	Due to the motorway links it has a very large sphere of influence. Drivers 60 miles away can get there in one hour.
P	Parking	A number of large, free car parks.
A	All-weather shopping	Better than the high street on a rainy day.
C	Choice of shops	Greater variety of shops.
E	Expansion	The large site allows for further expansion if required.
S	Secure	Security staff are on hand to help customers and deter criminals. These staff are not available in the high street.

Test Yourself

(a) Complete the following paragraph:

_____ order _____ describes goods bought almost every day. They are cheap and

people do not _____ far to buy them. _____ order _____ are bought less often

and are _____. People will travel _____ to buy them. The minimum number of people

required is called the _____ population. Shops or settlements arranged in a structure are

called a _____.

(b) List the characteristics of a CBD.

(c) Using 'CAR SPACES' to help you, list nine characteristics of an out-of-town shopping centre.

(d) Give four reasons why many people oppose out-of-town shopping centres.

Urban to rural migration in the UK

Some people, often the young, are leaving British villages as there are few facilities and not many local jobs, they can't afford to buy or rent local houses, and not much is going on. Many people are moving **to** villages to escape the noise, pollution and traffic of towns, preferring a quieter life in the countryside. They include retired people, but also those who live in the village and work in the towns. These people commute to work.

In many villages local people may support their local shops, bus services and community life. Some people live in the town but buy a second home, to visit only at weekends or in the summer. Such people contribute little to village life during the week or in winter. By buying a cottage they may be preventing local people doing so, or they push up the price of property in the area.

Townspeople who move to the village and commute to work in the city are there all year and in the evenings. They too can outbid local people for houses, but they often contribute to village life and can see areas for improvement. Sometimes they are busy people who start up village societies and campaign to protect wildlife. Notice how in places such as Thurston (see below) and villages like Cutnall Green and Cookley near Kidderminster, the arrival of new people from the cities does **not** save the local shops from closure. The newcomers continue to support the cheaper shops in their old town.

◀ *Figure 2.13 Stereotypes of traditional village dwellers and the newcomers. How true do you think they are?*

Find and visit a real village. You will not spot contrasting attitudes, but look for:
- modern housing estates
- converted farm buildings
- old cottages being modernised
- bus stops, or lack of them
- village shops or lack of them
- post office or lack of it
- prices of the houses.

Look for these trends in the example below.

Thurston is a village 14km from Bury St Edmunds in Suffolk. For many years it was an agricultural village with a small market. When the railway was built to Thurston in 1846, the market grew rapidly as produce could be sent more easily to towns and cities. Later, the railway brought commuters who lived in Thurston and worked in Bury St Edmunds. Thurston developed two sections: a farming village and a commuter village, with the church in between the two.

From 1950 onwards, as car ownership grew, many more people moved to the village. The gap between the two parts of the village was filled with new estates. Some newcomers travelled to London to work. Meanwhile, the number of farmworkers in the village declined. This was mainly due to mechanisation of work on the land.

At the same time, some businesses wanted to move into the village. The old grainstore by the station was converted into business units for small companies. Now, the rural nature of Thurston has disappeared. Most of the village shops have closed. People travel to the superstores on the edge of Bury St Edmunds for most of their shopping. The original local people find it difficult to buy property in the villages as the newcomers have forced up prices beyond farmworkers' incomes.

Examination Practice Question – foundation level paper

(a) Study Figure 2.14

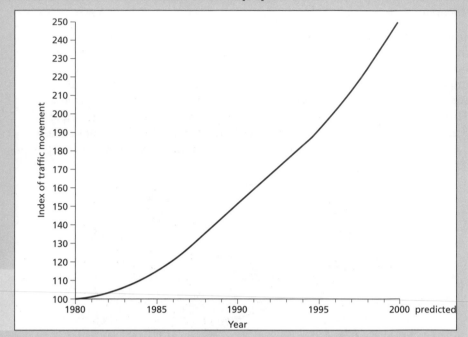

▶ *Figure 2.14 Traffic movement in the city of Cambridge*

The 'Index of Traffic Movement' is a measurement of traffic for every 100 vehicles in 1980.

(i)   In which year had the Index of Traffic Movement doubled to 200?   [1]

(ii) Give one reason for the increase in the amount of traffic in cities such as Cambridge?   [1]

(iii) Suggest three problems that would be caused by the increase in traffic in a city such as Cambridge.   [3]

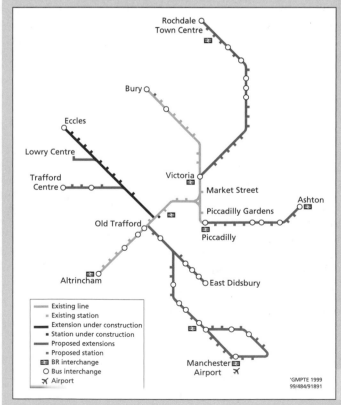

(b) Study Fig 2.15.

The Metrolink is a tramway system in a major British city.

Use evidence from the diagram to explain why extending the Metrolink network will make it easier to travel in and around this city.   [2]

(c) Describe some attempts that have been or are being made to improve the movement of people and goods in a town or city that you have studied.   [4]

◀ *Figure 2.15 Metrolink map*

Summary

Hints and Tips!
Case studies are worth 7 marks out of 19 in a question. The exercise at the bottom of this page is valuable in identifying the correct case studies, which should help you to score high marks in the exam.

Key words to know and understand

Birth rate	Inner city zones
Central business district	Integrated transport system
Death rate	Migration
Dependants	Population density
Green belts	Population structure
Hierarchy	Sphere of influence
Infant mortality rate	Suburbs

Check list for revision

	Understand and know	Needs more revision	Do not understand	Refer to pages
I know the reasons for the varied population densities.	☐	☐	☐	35
I understand why population structures vary from one country to another.	☐	☐	☐	36
I understand what the dependency ratio implies.	☐	☐	☐	37
I can give the reasons for population growth.	☐	☐	☐	38
I can quote the details of a major international migration.	☐	☐	☐	40
I can explain why people migrate within a country.	☐	☐	☐	42–43
I can describe strategies to improve the quality of life in squatter settlements.	☐	☐	☐	42–43
I know the differences between the characteristics of inner zones and suburban zones in the United Kingdom.	☐	☐	☐	45–46
I understand the different strategies in tackling traffic congestion in towns.	☐	☐	☐	48–49
I understand the attractions and problems of out-of-town shopping centres.	☐	☐	☐	51
I understand the impact of people moving to rural villages.	☐	☐	☐	47–48

Know your case studies

Which real places have you studied as an example of...

- Population control   name:_____ p 39
- International migration   name:_____ p 41
- Migration within a country name:_____ p 43
- CBD   name:_____ p 45
- Inner zones   name:_____ p 45
- Suburbs   name:_____ p 46
- Transport planning   name:_____ p 48
- Urban regeneration   name:_____ p 53

Unit 3: People and their needs

This unit looks at people's needs and in particular:
- the quality of life and how it varies between countries
- different types of employment
- tourism
- different sources of energy
- the effects of all these activities on the environment.

The quality of life

Key ideas
- Imbalances in the quality of life between countries.
- The employment structure as an indicator of economic development.
- The causes and consequences of rapid industrial growth of an LEDC.

Key words and definitions

Correlation	the connection between two factors.
Infant mortality	the number of children who die under the age of one year per 1,000 live births.
Literacy	percentage of adults who can read and write.
Nutrition	how much food a person eats, measured in calories. A person normally needs an intake of between 2,000 and 3,000 calories per day to remain healthy.
Primary industries	involve extracting minerals or food from the ground or sea.
Quality of life	how good life is in a country. Usually measured by objective factors such as wealth per person and life expectancy.
Secondary industries	processing of raw materials to make something.
Tertiary sector/ service sector	provide the other two industries with backup services, for example administration, banking and transport.

Imbalances between countries

The exam may ask you to compare overall trends of groups of countries and talk about two specific countries. How long you live is an important question! So too is the quality of your life. You cannot measure happiness but you can measure other aspects of life, e.g. wealth, education and health support etc.

Candidates in the higher paper answer *one* of the two questions provided. Candidates in the foundation paper have only one question provided.

Hints and Tips!

In this and the next unit you will be asked several times to refer to your own named examples or case studies. On each occasion take the trouble to find your own notes. Avoid vague answers: give the details requested and aim to pick up all the marks. The answer sections contain detailed answers for you if you don't have them, so check this section and see what you have missed. Experience shows that case studies local to you often provide better answers than a textbook example, provided you can give detailed answers that fit the question.

Learn what the following mean and what to look for in the exam:

Quality of life indicators	
GDP $ per head	This is the gross domestic product (the wealth a country produces), divided by the total population
Life expectancy	Notice that on average women live longer than men
Patients per doctor	Notice here that the lower the number the better things are
Education	In many countries parents have to pay for schooling. Often children receive 2 or 3 years' primary education but very few receive secondary education, and then usually boys only
Infant mortality	The number of infant deaths per 1,000 live births
Literacy	The ability of people to read and write
Nutrition	What people eat, and the adequacy of that food in terms of vitamins and minerals

Questions

Describe the effects that lack of education has on the development of a country.

A sample answer might be:
A workforce with little education probably has low reading skills. This makes it difficult to develop the skilled jobs which are more highly paid. These desirable jobs are often filled by foreign workers (from the USA, Japan, Europe etc.), leaving the local people to carry on farming or working in the low-status jobs. The development of IT activities, medical care etc. is usually in the hands of foreign companies, who 'control' growth.

There are links between the wealth of a country and the quality of life in those countries. Study Figure 3.1.

▼ *Figure 3.1 The links between the wealth of a country and quality of life*

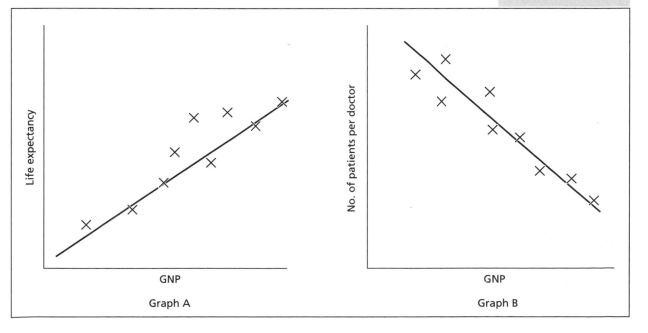

Note that each cross represents a country. The line of best fit goes through the middle of the cluster of crosses in graph A and there is a correlation (connection) between the two indicators. If the line goes in the / direction this is called a positive correlation. As the wealth goes up life expectancy goes up. In graph B there is a definite pattern but the line goes \. This is a negative correlation. Note there is a correlation, but as the wealth goes up in this example the number of patients per doctor goes down (this is good). Do not be misled into thinking that a negative correlation means no correlation. That is not true.

Questions

Explain why, as a country becomes wealthier, the average life expectancy goes up. To gain full marks you must list the main points and explain the links between them. One-phrase answers will not do.

Test Yourself

A sample answer might be: As a country becomes more wealthy, education improves → better paid jobs → better housing conditions → better diet → fewer diseases.

Governments can train more doctors/nurses, provide more clinics, afford more drugs etc. Eventually hospitals can provide very different operations, such as heart operations, hip replacements etc. Piped purified water can be supplied, rather than the old contaminated water from the local well.

Cover up the page.
Define
- Primary industry
- Secondary industry
- Tertiary industry

Employment structure as an indicator of economic development

Industry can be divided into three main sectors.
- Primary – concerned with farming, mining, quarrying and fishing – where something is extracted from the earth.
- Secondary – where the raw material is processed into a product or used as a fuel. Car factories, power stations and food canning are all secondary activities.
- Tertiary – this is the service sector. Industries here assist the others by providing finance, business advice and transport. No product is actually made in this sector. Education, the leisure industry and shops are all tertiary activities.

With few exceptions (e.g. some oil-producing countries and countries such as Australia) countries with mainly primary activities are considered less economically developed, whereas advanced countries have large tertiary sectors. Figure 3.2 shows the employment structure of a range of countries.

Notice how no country on the list has the secondary sector as the largest sector. Tertiary jobs and industries generally provide more wealth than primary sectors, especially if we are talking about farming. Agricultural products will never produce much wealth – too many other countries can grow those crops. Naturally every country wants to

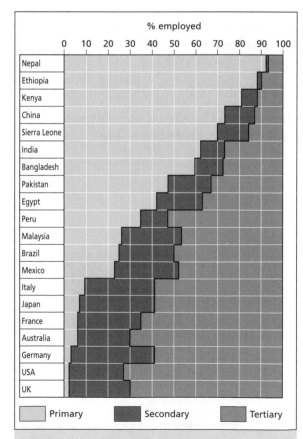

▲ Figure 3.2 Comparing employment structure

industrialise and then develop a tertiary sector: few countries can do so quickly, but they try.

Difficulties involved with developing secondary and tertiary sectors include:
- need for loans to finance development
- need for modern transport infrastructure
- need to educate young people and then train them in specific skills
- the natural reluctance of advanced countries to help poorer countries become rivals.

Reasons for rapid industrial growth in a less economically developed country
- LEDCs tend to be agricultural countries, perhaps still involved with shifting cultivation, subsistence farming and producing products such as rubber or cocoa (useful to make chocolate) under the control of foreign companies or countries. Economic growth is slow.
- Foreign companies are attracted to these countries, as wage rates are low. New factories are established.
- Once set up these new companies lead to other developments. Greater production encourages more roads to speed exports in transit, provides the local workforce with money so they spend more and so the economy develops rapidly. Some countries have been able to develop quickly, including the so-called tiger economies of southeast Asia. Growth rates of 6% per year or more have been achieved compared with a UK average of about 2% per year. Recently tiger economies have been hit by a slow down in world trade and also by problems caused by corruption and economic mis-management.

Hints and Tips!

You need one case study of an LEDC which has experienced rapid industrial growth. Be able to describe the causes and consequences of the rapid growth. Malaysia is an alternative to South Korea.

Know your case study

South Korea
Like other less developed countries the South Korean government realised that agricultural production was not the route to economic and wealth creation.

- It therefore encouraged foreign investment but also developed its own research and development of high-tech products.
- Large international firms (trans-national companies) brought valued know-how to South Korea and were attracted by low wages, weak unions, low taxes and nearby consumer markets such as China.
- South Korean firms were protected by high import taxes etc. Rapid economic growth of 6% led to it being recognised as a tiger economy.
- Despite a lack of its own iron ore South Korea became a shipbuilding country, taking over this role from Japan who had previously taken it over from Great Britain. Now in turn China is seeking to be the leading nation for shipbuilding. Notice the on-going process. Nothing remains static for long!
- The car industry was developed very rapidly. Most vehicles were exported as few South Koreans had the money to buy their own cars.
- The wheel comes almost full circle as South Korean electronics firms are now building factories in the USA and Europe! Look in your home and see how many products are made in South Korea, Malaysia and Taiwan.

Such rapid growth can only come at a price. Be ready in the exam to write about these problems. They could include:
- **Social** – unequal pay, use of child labour, sweat shop working conditions are all aspects of exploitation and can lead to social unrest and boycotting of goods by concerned consumers in advanced countries.

Case study *continued*

- **Environmental** – the pursuit of economic growth is often at the cost of a clean environment. Air and water pollution is often high in such countries as South Korea and Mexico. Increasingly we find polluting industries moving out of regulated countries like Britain and setting up in less regulated countries such as Mexico, South Korea and India.
- **Cultural** – employing women may upset long established cultural beliefs held by both men and women.
- **Economic** – poorer countries have become more tied to richer countries. When there is a downturn in world trade the poorer countries find themselves trapped in a situation they cannot control.

The interdependence of places

This cartoon illustrates the need to cooperate. If either man withdrew his umbrella both would drown. Similarly, although some countries are more advanced than others, no country can afford to go it alone.

- South Korea has an important place in world trade markets especially in high-tech products; therefore it is bound up with the success or otherwise of the Japanese, European and North American economies. A downturn in the American economy, leading to high unemployment in that country would mean fewer products being bought from South Korea by Americans.
- The changes around the world following the economic slow down in the USA in 2001 clearly illustrate the interdependence of countries in the modern world.
- Decisions in North America by the management of high-tech firms in South Korea could easily have a knock-on effect in South Korea and other Far East countries.

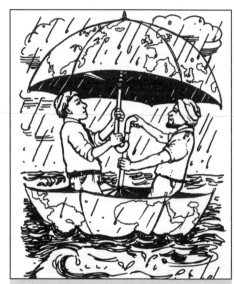

▲ *Figure 3.3 The interdependence of rich and poor countries*

Examination Practice Question – higher level paper

(a) Study Figure 3.4.

▼ *Figure 3.4*

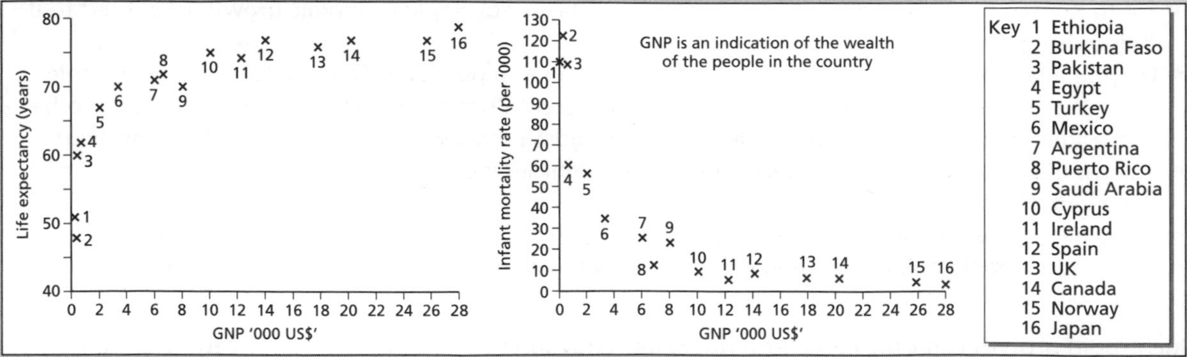

Life expectancy (years)
GNP '000 US$'
Infant mortality rate (per '000)
GNP is an indication of the wealth of the people in the country
Key
1 Ethiopia
2 Burkina Faso
3 Pakistan
4 Egypt
5 Turkey
6 Mexico
7 Argentina
8 Puerto Rico
9 Saudi Arabia
10 Cyprus
11 Ireland
12 Spain
13 UK
14 Canada
15 Norway
16 Japan

(i) In which country is the average life expectancy 67 years and the infant mortality rate 57 per 1,000? [1]

(ii) To what extent are the relationships shown on the two graphs different? Explain why they are different. [4]

Examination Practice Question – higher level paper *continued*

(b) Study Figure 3.5.

United Kingdom	Protein (g)	Calories	India	Protein (g)	Calories
Breakfast Cornflakes with milk and sugar Bacon and egg Toast and marmalade	22.1	595	**Breakfast** Rice cakes Banana	3.6	366
Lunch Fish, chips and peas Pudding and custard	28.4	970	**Lunch** Rice, beans, carrots, dried fish, onion and potatoes	26.1	628
Evening meal Beans and sausage, bread and butter Orange	17.6	689	**Evening meal** Rice, lentils, carrots and potatoes Buttermilk	12.5	511
Snacks Milk and biscuits Chocolates and crisps	14.0	560	**Snacks** None		
Total	**82.1**	**2814**	**Total**	**42.2**	**1505**

▲ *Figure 3.5 Diets of two 10-year-old children*

Oxfam recommends that the average 10-year-old needs about 80g of protein and 2,000 calories per day.

(i)   Why are diets likely to be so different in the two countries?   [3]

(ii) What will be the possible long-term effects of such diets on the quality of life of adults? [4]

(c) The quality of life of people may be affected by the development of manufacturing industry. Name and locate an industry that you have studied and describe how it has affected the local environment and people living nearby.   [7]

[Total 19 marks]

Economic activities

Key ideas
- Contrasts between commercial farming and subsistence farming.
- How farming is changing in the UK (or EU).
- Location of manufacturing and distribution industries.
- Effects of changing economic activity on communities.
- Effects of tourism.

Key words

Commercial farming	crops grown to sell for cash.
Diversification	moving into other activities. Not relying on one activity.
Intensive farming	where a lot of food is grown in a small area.

Location	where something (towns, factories etc) is placed.
Science Park	high-tech firms are often located in these, close to a university to enable co-operation and development.
Subsistence farming	where crops are grown just for the farmer and his family.

The interaction of factors affecting agricultural land

Environmental factors such as temperature, rainfall, amount of sunshine, quality and type of soil and steepness of slope have always been important in determining the type of agricultural activity to be carried out. Now, however, financial factors are becoming increasingly important.

Contrasts between commercial farming and subsistence farming

Know your case study

Dairy farming in North Yorkshire
Dairy farms in the UK still tend to be family run businesses.

Why dairy farming and not something else? In North Yorkshire there is:
- medium to heavy rain which encourages good pasture.
- heavy soil which make arable crops difficult to grow.
- some grass cut for use as silage (winter feed for the cattle when it is too cold for grass to grow in the fields).
- a ready market for milk either as milk or cheese.

Farmers were originally encouraged by government and EU subsidies to develop milk production. However, over production across much of Europe led to the introduction of milk quotas. Farmers were then *fined* for over production. The price paid for the milk has also been cut.

Many farmers are now leaving the business or finding additional sources of income – caravan sites, tourists experience farm-life etc. The climate has not changed that much but the economics and politics have.

Hints and Tips!

You will need to know two case studies here. One from the UK or EU and one from an LEDC.

Your case study may involve grain farmers in East Anglia. Here many hedgerows were removed to make large fields suitable for use by large combine harvesters etc. There was a significant loss of insect and bird life as the insects depended on the hedgerows for food. Soil erosion became worse as the winds that blew across the flat East Anglian landscape were no longer slowed down by hedges.

Subsistence farming

Subsistence farming is where farmers grow food for themselves and their families. A surplus is rare so there is no cash income to the farm. Intensive farming is where as high a yield as possible is obtained from a small piece of land. No land is wasted.

Know your case study

Intensive subsistence farming in the Ganges Valley, Bangladesh and northern India

- Climate: Rainfall is high – up to 2,000 mm a year in places – but it is mostly concentrated in the monsoon period between July and October.
- Temperatures are high and encourages rice-growing all year round. A shortage of water after October is a problem.
- Soil is fertile due to annual flooding of the river Ganges in the monsoon months.
- Crops: Rice, which has high nutritional value, forms more than 85% of the total diet in the Ganges valley. Padi (wet rice) needs the rich soil of the area and is planted while there is water on the ground as soon as the rains begin. It is harvested in October when the ground becomes dry. If irrigation (water brought to the fields in pipes and channels) has been developed, a second rice crop may be grown as it needs a growing season of only 100 days. Millet, maize, wheat and barley are additional crops grown in the area.
- Organisation: Farming is labour intensive. Many people are needed, as few machines are available. Tasks include weeding, ploughing to break the soil, planting, harvesting and developing irrigation systems.
- Farm size: Often as small as 1 hectare (the size of a football pitch). The high population in the Ganges valley leads to very small farms per family. It takes 2,000 hours a year to look after just 1 hectare.
- Farm ownership: Many farmers are only tenants. They do not control the farm or benefit from any developments to it. Innovation is therefore slow.
- Supportive power: Water buffalo help with the work. Manure is used as a fuel not as fertiliser.
- Marketing: Rare with subsistence farming. Poor roads hinder the sale of any surplus rice in good years.
- Recent changes: New varieties of rice and wheat have been specially developed for poorer regions. Yields increased but so did the demand for tractors and fertilisers putting new burdens on the farmers.

Summary

Feature	United Kingdom (Commercial)	Ganges Valley (Subsistence)
Climate	Temperatures 3–18°C. Rainfall throughout the year, 500mm to 1500mm	High temperature (20–30°C). Monsoon rainfall for part of year
Soil	Various	Fertile soil due to flooding
Crops	Wheat, barley etc. in East Anglia. Grass for animals in west	Mainly rice
Organisation	1 owner. A few labourers	Labour intensive. Few machines
Farm size	Often 300 hectares	1 hectare
Farm ownership	Farmer or by commercial organisation	Tenants
Supportive power	Tractors etc.	Buffalo
Marketing	On contract to large firms	Rare
Change	Diversification into other activities due to EU action	Some new strains of rice

42 People and their needs

How farming is changing in the UK and the EU

- The current face of farming is shaped by policies begun just after the Second World War. Britain had nearly been starved into surrender and much of Europe faced food shortages. If this seems incredible to you, then it shows how successful the policies have been since that time.
- The British landscape in 1950 was the result of farming practices in the Middle Ages modified by the enclosures of the eighteenth century. All of this in an age of human and animal power with very few tractors. Fields were fairly small, often irregular in shape and surrounded by trees *and* hedges, which supported a rich and varied wildlife. Many farmers kept animals and grew crops – this is called mixed farming.

▼ *Figure 3.6 Field sketches of a farm in 1949 and 2000*

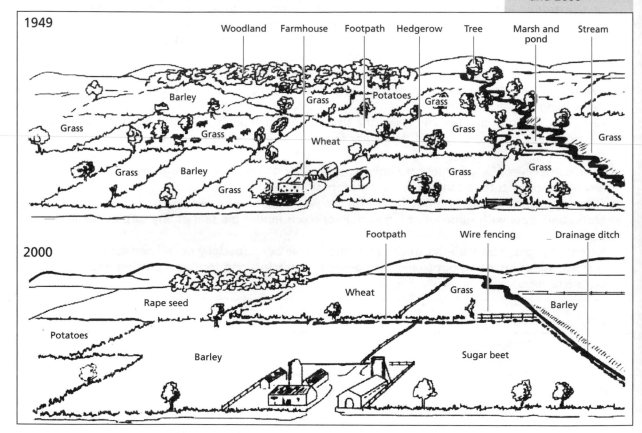

- Normally the farmer would consider such environmental factors as slope, rainfall, temperature, labour and transport costs and the sale price of the produce when deciding what to produce. However, the financial aid, financial penalties and the government regulations of Britain and the EU have become the chief influences on farmers since 1945.
- Since that time British farmers were encouraged to produce enough food so that the country was virtually self-sufficient in all but tropical foodstuffs. Wet lands were drained and many hedges removed to allow for the costly combine harvesters and other machines, which required large regular shaped fields in order to be economic. Between 1980 and 1995 average farms increased from 70 to 95 hectares.
- After Britain joined the EU in 1973 it adopted the Common Agricultural Policy which further encouraged greater production. Because of the power of farmers in Europe, all farmers in the EU were guaranteed prices for their produce however much they grew or however many animals they reared. This led to overproduction. Surplus milk was stored

in the form of butter. Cereals and beef were stored in costly warehouses. Far too much cheap wine was produced and was often thrown away once the farmer and the wine company had been paid. By the mid-1980s (with 70% of the EU money going on farming, which provided only 5% of the EU's income) something had to be done.

- **Milk quotas.** Farmers were rationed as to how much milk they could produce from their farms. They were *fined* if they produced too much milk. This led to many dairy herds being reduced and the farmers turning to beef cattle or wheat production.
- Further changes were still needed so in 1992 **set aside** was introduced. Farmers were *paid* to leave fields empty, or planted with trees or used for non-farming purposes such as a caravan site.
- In 1995 subsidies for cereal crops were reduced but those for oilseed rape increased. (This is the yellow-coloured crop now so common in the countryside. It has high cooking oil content, something that the EU was short of.)

- Notice how farmers have responded to the prompting of the politicians and their subsidies in their drive to produce more food. AGRIBUSINESS is a term to describe the industrialisation of farming (often at the expense of the environment).
- With the increasing cost of EU farming and its over production there is a growing demand for more thought to be given to environmental factors. The disasters of BSE and the Foot and Mouth outbreaks in 2001 are encouraging demands for better *quality* food (not more quantity), even if that means higher prices. The virtual closure of much of Britain's countryside in 2001 cost the tourist industry more than the farmers. A reappraisal of priorities is happening. Read newspaper articles and watch the TV for the latest developments in farming including **organic farming**, which is the growing of crops without using chemical fertilisers.

Changes in the EU

From your school notes, try this exam question then look at the answers at the back of the book. Learn any items that you have missed out.

Examination Practice Question – higher level paper

(a) Study Figure 3.6 on page 64.

  (i) Identify two changes in the farming landscape which have taken place between 1949 and 2000.   [2]

  (ii) Explain why the farming landscape has changed between these two years. Do not restrict your answer only to the changes identified in part (i) of this question.   [5]

Set aside
Quotas
Subsidies
Diversification

(b) Study Figure 3.7 on the left. Describe how EU policies such as those in the figure can affect a farmer's decision making.   [4]

(c) Identify the difference between a commercial farming system and a subsistence farming system. [2]

◀ *Figure 3.7 EU policies*

Location of industry in the UK

Geographers are always interested in patterns, especially those that change. Industry has changed its location and the reasons for that location in the last 100 years.

Originally in the 1800s and early 1900s industry located where the raw materials – coal and iron ore etc. – were found. These were heavy and expensive to transport, so it was cheaper to locate near them than to transport them a long way to a factory. The industrial belts of South Wales, the Black Country of the Midlands, Yorkshire and Lancashire, the North East and Central Scotland developed for this reason.

Know your case study

The Pottery Industry – Stoke-on-Trent

This is the story of an industry that began because of local raw materials but then became such an important industry that it survived the exhaustion of those materials. The needs of the pottery industry led to an improvement of the region's transport which is still important today.

- The industry began due to local supplies of clay and marl which were used to produce low-quality tiles and earthenware pipes.
- Coal from the north Staffordshire coalfield was used to heat kilns in which the pottery was placed to 'fire' the products.
- Due to the inventiveness and persistence of Josiah Wedgwood other raw materials were brought to the region to improve the quality of the clay. Ball clay from Dorset, china clay from Cornwall, and bones (for bone china) came from Argentina.
- Transport was rather poor so Josiah Wedgwood encouraged the building of the Trent-Mersey Canal so that the raw materials could be imported and the finished fragile pottery could be exported safely.
- In the 1970s, 75% of pottery employees in Britain worked in Stoke.
- Today the industry has developed a wide range of products including items for the electricity industry (pottery does not conduct electricity).
- Much pottery is expensive due to the quality of the clay and the skills of the designers and craftspeople. As such, the industry is subject to changes in demand as fashions change and the impact of foreign competition.

Several factories have now closed and the towns around Stoke-on-Trent are looking to diversify into other industries.

Hints and Tips!

You will need two case studies here, one of a manufacturing industry and one of a distribution industry. Both **must** be in the UK.

Know your case study

Alcan Smelter, Lynemouth

This is a modern example of heavy industry being guided to a particular location.

Aluminium is made from bauxite found in Australia and Jamaica so why isn't the smelter in those countries? The main factor in the location of an aluminium smelter is a cheap and plentiful supply of electricity. Lynemouth has extensive supplies of coal so the smelter was built next to the coal-fuelled power station.

Case study *continued*

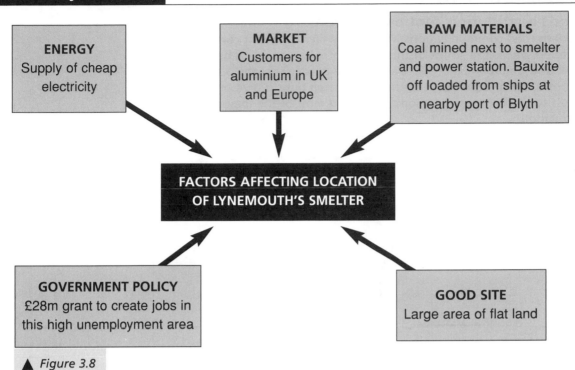

ENERGY
Supply of cheap electricity

MARKET
Customers for aluminium in UK and Europe

RAW MATERIALS
Coal mined next to smelter and power station. Bauxite off loaded from ships at nearby port of Blyth

FACTORS AFFECTING LOCATION OF LYNEMOUTH'S SMELTER

GOVERNMENT POLICY
£28m grant to create jobs in this high unemployment area

GOOD SITE
Large area of flat land

▲ *Figure 3.8*

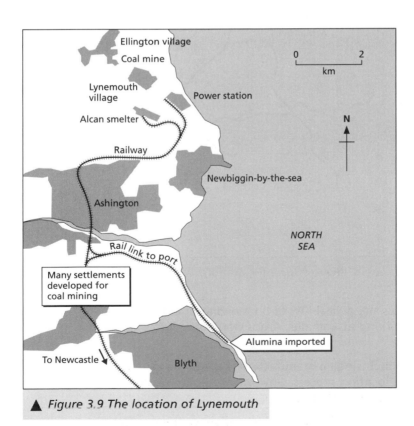

▲ *Figure 3.9 The location of Lynemouth*

If the *coal mine* closed the whole project would carry on. The power station could be fed by oil/gas. When factories and industries stay in the same place it is called *industrial inertia*.

Argos distribution centre in Stafford

Modern road communications was the key factor when it came to deciding where the Argos distribution centre was going to be based. Look at the map in Figure 3.10 and notice how central the Stafford centre is. Despite the fact that the M6 is often busy, it gives motorway access to the company's regional bases and most of the major centres of population.

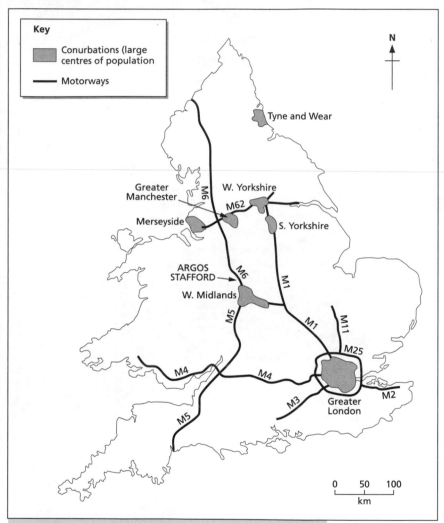

▲ Figure 3.10 Location of the Argos centre, Stafford

The other factor was the availability of a trained local labour force who were previously working at a smaller Argos warehouse just 5 km away at Penkridge.

Notice that no product is being manufactured here so no raw materials are influencing the location process. Government policy was not a factor this time, although it quite often is.

The above are called *location* factors, which influence the general area to be chosen. Below are the *site* factors, which influence the exact spot to be chosen.

Case study *continued*

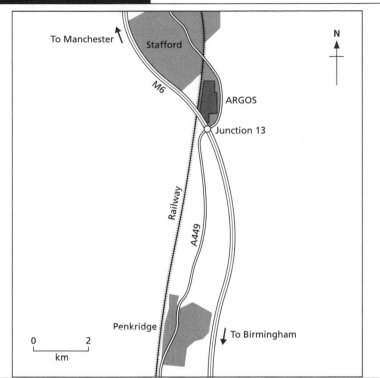

▲ *Figure 3.11 The site of Argos distribution centre, Stafford*

Hints and Tips!

For your case studies be really clear why both the site and the situation were chosen. The spot was not chosen by accident.

Site factors usually include:

- Slope – here the ground was flat.
- Size – here the site was small and does not allow for expansion.
- Type of ground – the Argos site was a greenfield site, i.e. it had never been built on before. Brownfield sites have been built on before and may be costly to clear before new building can start.
- Surrounding features – roads and other fields are next to the Argos site. Sometimes there are factories, houses, canals, railways etc. that influence location decisions.

Today electricity or gas provides the energy required, so many industries are free to go where they please (the so-called footloose industries). Most are now influenced by where their skilled workforce is found and sometimes the government offers financial aid for industry to locate in areas of high unemployment. Modern road communications assist in the delivery of the final product, and are therefore a location factor.

Effects of tourism

In the 1950s a British family holiday was often a week at a British seaside and that was it! Since then the increase in paid holidays, the development of jet aircraft which provides cheap holidays over long distances, TV and the thirst for travel have led to radical changes in the leisure industry.

Tourism undoubtedly brings many benefits, such as jobs, new money and improvements to the area, but it also brings its problems, including a dependency on wealthy countries and threats to the environment and local culture.

Historic sites in Europe, such as in Greece, Crete and Italy, 'suffer' from tourism even though local people gain from the tourists spending money on:
- hotels
- guides
- entrance fees to sites
- souvenirs etc.
- food.

The damage can happen in a variety of ways:
- Deliberate theft of items from a site (1000 tourists, each one taking a tiny piece of stone from Pompeii, for example, can cause noticeable damage).
- Footpaths can become so worn and polished as to be potentially dangerous. (Although it is not a historic site, visitors to Dovedale in Derbyshire will remember the highly polished stones of that particular footpath.)
- Grassy areas soon become destroyed by the constant trampling.
- The tourist coaches and cars cause air pollution, which is chemically eating away at the ancient buildings. The stone frieze from the Parthenon which is currently stored in London's British Museum is in better shape than the Parthenon itself in Athens.
- Some old buildings are being damaged by traffic vibration.
- Many historic sites are not in easily accessible areas. Roads and footpaths are sometimes built for the benefit of tourists, but at a cost to the appearance of the local environment.
- Sometimes an area can become cluttered with tourist gift shops.
- Flash photography can cause tremendous damage over the years. Cave paintings in southern France and classic medieval paintings in Italy are no longer on show to the public so as to preserve them for scientific and artistic appreciation. Copies are sometimes displayed for those who are interested.

Stop and Think

On balance, do you think tourism is a good or bad thing for an area or country?

Hints and Tips!
You need a case study of the effects of tourism in Europe but **not** the UK.

Know your case study

Menorca: a popular Spanish holiday island
Menorca is a popular tourist venue because:

- summers are hot, dry and very sunny.
- flights from Britain take 2 hours, so it is not surprising that three-quarters of the tourists are British.

Increased tourism resulted in:

- many jobs related to the tourist industry being developed, e.g. the making and selling of postcards and souvenirs.

- outsiders buying villas on the island. This caused resentment amongst the locals similar to that caused by towns people moving into villages in Britain (see page 53).
- many beautiful areas being spoilt by hotels which sprang up in an uncontrolled way.

The Spanish government has now sought to control the worst excesses of tourism by:

- limiting further development
- restricting the height of new buildings
- restricting ownership of property on the island
- promoting the local language and culture.

The government is attempting to enjoy the benefits of tourism whilst restricting the harmful effects.

What do you think should be the ideal balance?

Hints and Tips!

Use these answers opposite if there is a question on the management of tourism.

Know your case study

Kenya: a less economically developed country making progress through tourism

The reason that you need to study **two** examples of tourism is that the impact of tourism is greater on less developed countries as they often have poor roads, tiny airports, low incomes, sometimes no system of regular and dependable water, sewerage or electricity supply. They do have a culture of their own which can be threatened by tourism. Be aware of all these factors when you do your studies.

- Mass tourism to places like Kenya and the West Indies is recent.
- It developed as people grew bored of Mediterranean holidays and wanted something different.
- The growing popularity of a gap year just before or after university, TV holiday programmes and certain films all combine to encourage people to experience something different.

Why Kenya?
- Sunshine all the year round.
- Wild animals in their natural surroundings.
- Beach resorts on the east coast.
- A very different culture.

Benefits to Kenya?
- More better quality roads.
- Improvements to the airports and hotels.
- Improved water and other utility supplies in some areas.
- All the year round jobs for Kenyan people (many of whom had been farmers before tourism arrived).

Drawbacks?
- Many people were tempted away from farming self-sufficiency to a better paid but less certain tourist industry.
- Many jobs are unskilled and so low paid by our standards.
- Tremendous damage to the safari environment.

Hints and Tips!

You need a case study of the good and bad effects of tourism in an LEDC.

Hints and Tips!

Be ready to describe a holiday picture. Look at the attractions of the place and also the effects that tourism is having on that location. Practise with holiday brochures.

Case study *continued*

- Resentment from some local people at the wealth of the visiting tourists. (Where have you heard this before and how do you feel when wealthy people visit your town or favourite holiday resorts?)
- Not all tourists are sympathetic to local but different cultures. Also local people are drawn in to dance for or provide objects for the tourists and in this way their culture can be devalued.

Flavour of the month

Just as the Mediterranean was **the** fashionable area (then Africa and the Far East), now Australia and Florida are very popular. Tourists are very fickle and an area can drop out of favour even at a moment's notice so countries that rely on tourism are taking a calculated risk.

Do not feel guilty when travelling abroad. Enjoy your holiday but be sensitive to the local environment and people.

Energy

This section looks at the changes in fuel type over the last 15–20 years. It then examines the human cost of those changes.

Key ideas
- Why is the relative importance of fossil fuels, nuclear power and alternative energy sources changing?
- What are the consequences for communities as the energy budget changes?

Key words and definitions

Alternative energy sources	renewable, environmentally friendly ways of creating energy e.g. wind power.
Fossil fuels	fuels such as coal, gas and oil created by plants and sea creatures millions of years ago.
Multiplier effect	this can be positive or negative. A new business coming into the area brings new money into the local economy. A business that closes also affects local suppliers and shops in a negative way.
Non-renewable fuels	fuels which can only be used once. Fossil fuels are non-renewable.
Renewable fuels	energy sources such as wind power and solar energy, which are created in nature every day.

The relative and changing importance of fossil fuels, nuclear power and alternative energy sources

Some fuels are used directly for energy; some to produce electricity.

Coal, gas and oil are all called fossil fuels as they originated from plants/trees and creatures that lived millions of years ago. Once used, they are **not** renewable.

Coal

Across the UK and Europe, the coal industry has suffered a massive decline in popularity. In the last century coal was used to heat homes and factories, was burnt in steam engines and used to generate electricity. Britain still has massive quantities of coal, but it is seen as a dirty, polluting and expensive

Hints and Tips!

Restrict your studies on changing fuel types to the UK only.

fuel (see the section on greenhouse gases and global warming in Unit 4). At present most coal is used in power stations, where it is burned to produce electricity. These power stations are usually near rivers, as vast quantities of water (which is turned into steam) are used to turn the turbines and the generators.

Oil

Oil is a more convenient fuel, being cleaner, easier to control and transport than coal but it too creates pollution in the form of acid rain. Britain has at least 50 years' reserves of oil, so continuity of supply is ensured for a while. Some believe the oil should be used for purposes other than producing electricity, as other less versatile fuels can be used for this purpose.

Natural gas

This fuel has become very popular not only to heat our homes and factories, but also as a source of fuel in power stations. It is clean (producing fewer greenhouse gases than other fuels), cheaper and generally easy to use. In the 1990s the government pursued a 'dash for gas' policy in its power stations at the expense of the coal industry. This meant that instead of maintaining a mixed fuel policy, the government brought in gas-fired stations. The economic and social needs of the coal miners were largely ignored. The big Didcot coal-fired power station west of London now uses gas for three-quarters of its fuel. In the 1980s the government had long feared the ability of miners to take industrial action, so it preferred the more mechanised, more 'reliable' gas industry.

Nuclear power

Nuclear power stations use very little fuel and nuclear power was once seen as the fuel of the future. However, worries about safety and the rising cost of this method of production have led to its decline in popularity with the government.

Examination Practice Question – higher level paper

a) Study Figure 3.13.

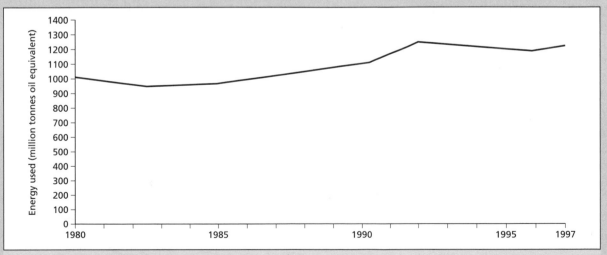

▲ Figure 3.13 Energy used in Europe

(i) How much energy was used in 1997? [1]

(ii) Describe the changes in the amount of energy used between 1980 and 1997. Support your answer with dates and figures. [4]

Continued

b) Study Figure 13.4.

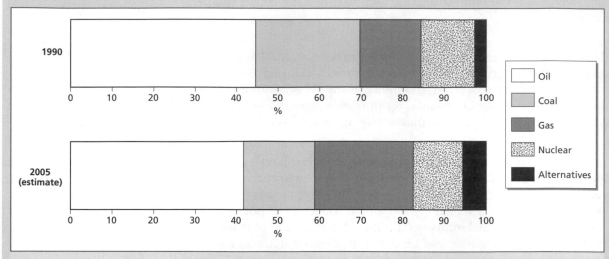

▲ *Figure 3.14 Types of energy used in Europe in 1990 and 2005 (estimate)*

(i) Describe the main changes in the use of energy as shown in Figure 13.14.   [3]

(ii) Suggest reasons why the importance of different types of energy may change by 2005.
     You should give at least three reasons and develop the points that you make.   [5]

Hints and Tips!

Be careful when reading bar charts, e.g. coal
consumption in 1990 is 25% not 69%.

Alternative energy sources

Apart from fossil fuels and nuclear power there
are some renewable (or sustainable) sources of
energy that cause little or no pollution. At
present most are in their trial stages and
currently do not provide much electricity to the
national grid.

Hydroelectric power (HEP)

Electricity can be produced by using the flow of
water to turn turbines and generators. In Britain
the amount produced in this way has remained
at about 0.5% for 40 years. Although a non-
polluting source, the number of rivers that have
a constant annual flow of sufficient quantity is
limited.

Wind power

An environmentally friendly source of energy
but still controversial. Currently 0.25% of UK
energy is generated in this way – some say 10%
is a possible total in the future.

▼ *Figure 3.12 Sketch
showing how a wind
power station changes
the landscape*

The turbines are constructed in groups of 25 or more in order to justify the transmission lines carrying electricity away to the towns.

High, exposed windy sites are clearly necessary. In turn this means they are easily seen. Some object to this 'visual pollution'. There is no air pollution but they do make a noise. Once constructed, they are cheap to run.

Many wind farms are needed to supply a small town, so there is a limit to the proportion of the nation's electricity that will come from this source.

Solar power and tidal power
Both are attractive sources owing to the low running costs, but they will not be viable sources of energy in the UK for many years – certainly not in the space of your exam course!

Consequences for communities as the energy budget changes
There is more to a mine or factory closure than demolishing a building. The livelihood, dreams and morale of the people in the area are also affected. Sometimes economic change can be positive, bringing new hope, but change good or bad has unseen effects on the local people. As the balance of fuel use changes there are social as well as economic costs.

Look up your case study on the social consequences of closure of a power source and look for comparisons with the example below. Look for the effects of the multiplier. This is where a new employer comes to an area. The wages paid to the employees are spent in local shops, creating or supporting yet more jobs. This is the positive multiplier. The problem comes when an employer pulls out. Local shops suffer as the employees of the firm have little or no money to spend. This is called the negative multiplier. In both cases the effects of extra money coming to an area, or a source of money drying up, are multiplied throughout a community. There is a knock-on effect.

> *Hints and Tips!*
> This section requires a case study from any MEDC.

▼ *Figure 3.15 The decline of coal mining in Nottinghamshire*

Know your case study

Coal mine closures in Nottinghamshire
In 1981, there were 161 collieries in England, employing 200,000 people. In 1998, only 20 remain employing around 10,000 people. In Nottinghamshire itself 35,000 miners' jobs were lost from 1980 onwards. Businesses linked to mining, such as mining engineering companies, were also affected.

- The main concern is that there is little alternative employment. Half of the miners at Silverhill Colliery, for example, were still unemployed one year later. Many do find jobs but they are low skill, low-paid jobs. Switching from a highly paid, physically tough, dirty job and moving into a low-paid typing job in an office is very difficult.

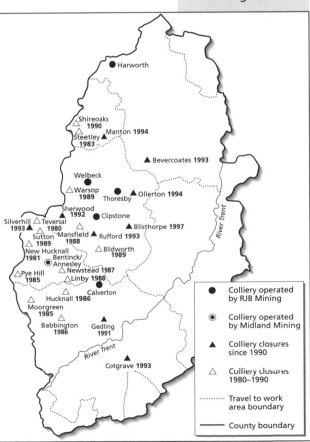

Case study *continued*

- Women take a lot of the jobs available. This can cause some problems for the men who have to rely on their wives, whereas in the past the men provided for the women. Today, equality of opportunity is paramount but many ex-miners find the changes hard to take. Pride and self-worth are important to these men.
- The mining villages were undoubtedly communities fostered through the adversity of mining. Now the pits have closed, the community sometimes finds it hard to stay together.
- Local shops have experienced difficulties. With the mines gone there is less money to be spent in the shops (see negative multiplier on earlier pages).
- Houses become difficult to sell. Few people want to move to an area with poor job prospects.
- Young people might not see any future in the area and either stop trying at school or want to move out to somewhere more prosperous.
- The area can become depressed in these circumstances.
- Many marriages come under pressure. Morale can be low and finances very difficult.
- The closure of a pit can lead to the disintegration of the whole village community.

Summary

Check list for revision

	Understand and know	Needs more revision	Do not understand	Refer to pages
I understand scatter graphs.	☐	☐	☐	57
I understand positive correlation.	☐	☐	☐	58
I understand that negative correlation does not mean there is no correlation.	☐	☐	☐	58
I can give detailed answers showing the differences between commercial and subsistence farming.	☐	☐	☐	63
I understand the factors affecting industrial location in the past.	☐	☐	☐	66
I can give details of the factors affecting modern industrial locations.	☐	☐	☐	66–69
I understand the good and bad effects of tourism.	☐	☐	☐	70–72
I realise economic change has significant effects.	☐	☐	☐	59
I understand the changes in energy supply sources.	☐	☐	☐	74
I can explain the social consequences of shutting a coal mine/power station.	☐	☐	☐	75

Know your case studies

Which real places have you studied as an example of...
- Rapid industrialisation   name:_____   p 59
- Commercial farming   name:_____   p 62
- Subsistence farming   name:_____   p 63
- Changes in farming in an MEDC   name:_____   p 64–65
- Manufacturing industry   name:_____   p 66
- Distribution industry   name:_____   p 68
- Problems caused by tourism in the EU (not the UK)   name:_____   p 70
- Problems caused by tourism in an LEDC   name:_____   p 71
- Effects on local villages of the closure of an energy source (coal mine/power station)   name:_____   p 75

Unit 4: People and the environment

All actions have consequences. In the past people have not always been aware of or concerned about the effect their actions have had on their surroundings. Today this is no longer the case.

Resource development and the local environment

Key ideas
- The environmental costs of mining and quarrying.

Key words and definitions
Open cast mining   Mining carried out at the surface in huge quarries
Overburden   Unwanted rock overlying valuable minerals such as coal

Extraction of raw materials, conflicts and attitudes
One case study from an MEDC is required here. Ensure you have all the details. No one likes a landscape spoiled by mining or quarrying, but without stone, coal or china clay, you would not have your house, roads or, maybe, any heating. We, the customers, need what is extracted. The quarry owners are just doing a job, like you or me.

Candidates in the higher paper answer *one* of the two questions provided. Candidates in the foundation paper have only one question provided.

Hints and Tips!

This unit has fewer sections to learn so your choice of topics will be limited. Learn all sections thoroughly to ensure that you can answer the selected question.

Know your case study

Limestone quarrying in the Peak District National Park

Extraction
- Limestone is one rock that helps to make the countryside attractive. The quarries themselves are unsightly with the grey quarries creating an obvious scar on the landscape which is normally green. Dust is created during the mining and processing stages and this is also unattractive.
- In Derbyshire itself, about 20 million tonnes of limestone are extracted every year.

Conflicts
- Walkers and country lovers clearly resent damage caused to the appearance of the landscape.
- Local residents also object to the number of lorries leaving and entering the quarries every day.
- Mine owners point out that jobs are created in this way and that local and national government benefit from the wealth and extra tax revenue created.
- Around Ladybower reservoir, Derbyshire, 400,000 tonnes of limestone are being extracted, creating more visual damage, but the stone is being used to support the dam of the reservoir and is generally seen as the best way to preserve the landmark and the reservoir behind it.

Opportunities
- Limestone workings were in existence before National Parks were created in 1946.
- Although requests for new quarries are monitored by the authorities, their value is such that no one intends to shut down the industry.

Case study *continued*

- Limestone is used for fertiliser (useful for farmers) and for building stone and cement (necessary for constructing the buildings we live in and the roads we use).
- Some stone is taken out by railway – more environmentally friendly than by lorry.
- Local authorities usually insist that closed quarries be landscaped as far as possible.
- Sometimes the quarries are flooded and converted to watersports centres.

Values and attitudes of people involved
- For quarry owners and their employees, limestone working provides jobs and profit. As much as 10% of male employment in Derbyshire is provided by mining and quarrying.
- Local residents object to large, noisy lorries working out of the quarry.
- Country lovers would much prefer unspoilt green countryside.
- Local government representatives have a balanced view of the situation. Quarries provide money for local government as well as jobs.
- National Park officers want to limit expansion of quarries. They will also want to see the quarry landscaped once workings have finished.

The amount of coal extracted in this country is now small. Some is mined from deep pits and some from opencast mines as shown in Figure 4.1. Notice how huge excavators called walking draglines remove the waste rock overburden which allows ordinary sized excavators to remove the coal.

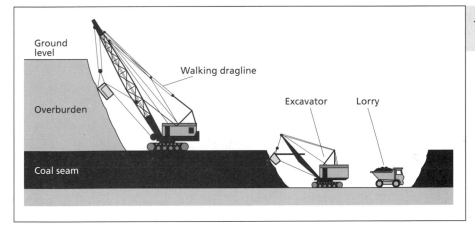

Figure 4.1 An opencast coal mine

Hints and Tips!

You need *one* case study example even though two are provided you for in this section.

Know your case study

Opencast mining at Smotherfly in Derbyshire
- The site covered 200 hectares and had reserves of 1,700,000 tonnes of coal. The overburden (topsoil and rock that was not coal) was removed first by a giant machine. Smaller machines then worked down into the ground, creating a hole 87 metres deep.
- The working was open to the sky at all times, so the dust problem had to be tackled. During mining operations the nearby River Erewash was diverted. The mine is now closed, the river follows its old course again, and every effort was made to restore the appearance of the land.
- Eighty jobs were created at this site, so while it was open about £4 million a year was put into the local economy in wages.
- The coal went to local power stations, thus reducing the need for expensive imports.

The management of environments

Key ideas
- Tropical rain forests have distinctive vegetation and wildlife which can be easily destroyed by human activity.
- National parks are valued by different groups for different reasons.
- The causes and effects of pollution of a river, lake or sea.

Hints and Tips!

Having looked at the problems caused to the environment, you now need to look at some attempts to manage them. Sometimes there are no easy, obvious answers. You need to know about both the problems and the options. You will not need to make the decisions yourself!

Key words and definitions

Biodiversity	the great variety of plants and animals.
Ecosystem	a method of showing how climate, soil, plants, insect and animal life all fit together.
Global warming	the steady rise in the earth's temperature.
Honeypots	specific villages or beauty spots that attract hundreds or thousands of tourists (like bees around a honeypot).
Industrial pollution	the effects may include rising sea levels and changes in climate world wide.
Landscaped	restoring old quarries so that the area looks similar to how it was before quarrying or mining began.
Leaching	where minerals in the soil are washed deep into the soil by heavy rain.
National Parks	areas of countryside protected by law from unwanted development. These are some of the best landscapes in a county.
Raw materials	the ingredients needed by industry (or farming) to make a product. Limestone rock is a raw material.

The fragile nature of the tropical rain forest ecosystem

Look at Figure 4.2, which shows the location of tropical rain forests. The tropics is where the sun is directly overhead at some point of the year. This means temperatures are high. Where there is plenty of rain as well then tropical rain forest will grow in profusion. With rainfall of 2000 mm and temperatures between 26° and 28°C every day of the year, trees up to 50 metres tall are common.

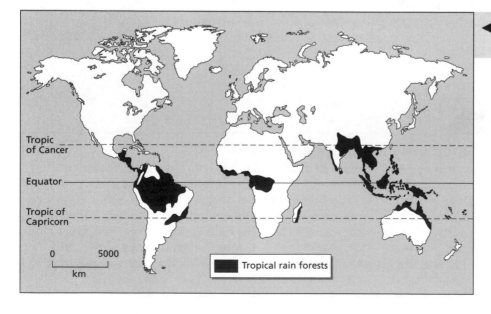

Figure 4.2 Location of tropical rain forests

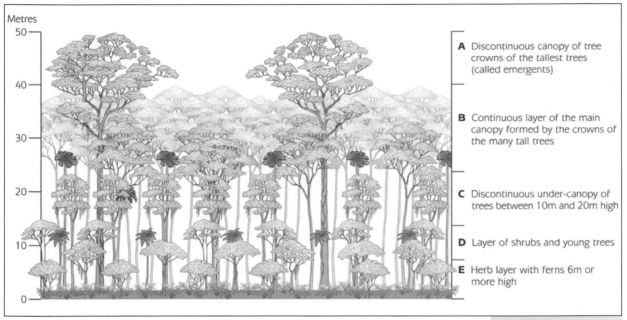

A Discontinuous canopy of tree crowns of the tallest trees (called emergents)

B Continuous layer of the main canopy formed by the crowns of the many tall trees

C Discontinuous under-canopy of trees between 10m and 20m high

D Layer of shrubs and young trees

E Herb layer with ferns 6m or more high

▲ *Figure 4.3 Layers of the rain forest*

Figure 4.3 shows the distinctive layers within the forests. Note especially the canopy layer 30 metres above ground, and the emergent layer 50 metres above ground.

The soils of the forest are not rich but are fed by leaf fall, which happens all year (there is no cooling of the air in autumn as we know it – there is no autumn!). The nutrients in the leaves are taken into the soil, then taken in by the tree and thus recycled.

If the trees are cut down, the cycle is broken. Nutrients do not replenish top soil and the loss of leaves and branches means more water reaches the ground. This in turn leads to leaching (the downward movement of minerals in the soil).

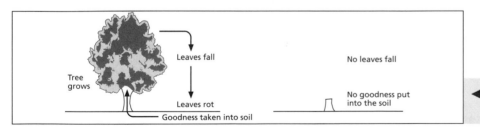

Tree grows

Leaves fall

Leaves rot

Goodness taken into soil

No leaves fall

No goodness put into the soil

◀ *Figure 4.4 Cycle of nutrients*

Any crops grown on the cleared lands take goodness out and so the land deteriorates even further. Two years of crops is all the land can produce, then it must be left fallow (empty) for several years to recover. Local tribes know this well and move around creating new areas for cultivation every couple of years. At the new site the trees are cut then burnt, so the ash gives extra nutrients to the soil for a while – the so-called 'slash and burn' technique.

On a small scale this works. However, as the indigenous (local) population grows and outsiders arrive in large numbers this delicate balance is being threatened. Soil erosion is the inevitable result.

Outside developers are rapidly clearing vast tracts of forest – for example mining companies seeking iron ore, gold and other minerals; multinationals creating grazing grounds for cattle; water companies and road builders etc.

DID YOU KNOW?

Despite the variety of trees and plants and the great amounts of foliage, the soils are very poor and need the leaf fall to stay fertile.

Local consequences of change

In addition to the breakdown of the nutrient cycle outlined above, there are other local consequences of deforestation:

- Animals and insects lose their habitats – 50% of all life forms are found in the rain forest adding up to an estimated 30 million species of plants, animals and insects.
- Soil erosion – research on the tropical forest reserve island of Maraca, Brazil, showed how important the mixture of roots and leaves on the ground is in checking soil erosion. Once trees are cut down the leaf supply stops and the roots that held the soil together die. Under the torrential rain of these areas unprotected soil is easily washed away.
- Local climate changes – as more water escapes down the rivers there is reduced evaporation and so less rain falls leading even to desertification!

Global consequences of deforestation

1. The oxygen balance. Trees take in carbon dioxide (which we breathe out) and 'breathe' out oxygen. Possibly one-third of the world's oxygen supply comes from rainforest trees, so if the forests were cleared there could be an oxygen shortage; this is unlikely.
2. Burning all the trees could increase the amount of carbon dioxide in the air, adding to the greenhouse effect. Forest burning in Brazil adds about 10% of all CO_2 to the atmosphere.
3. Deforestation results in less evapotranspiration, so rainfall will possibly be lower in the former rainforest areas.

There are countless different species of plants, trees, insects etc. in the rain forests. This biodiversity will be lost if the rainforests go. Also, many rainforest plants contain substances used in medicine.

What can be done? Stewardship and sustainable development

Stewardship implies that you do not own something for ever, but you have it for a while then pass it on.

Sustainable development is all about development which does not destroy the environment but nurtures it and allows continuing development. Recycling can play an important role here.

The Brazilian government has developed its economy despite the damage to the rain forest but has pointed to similar damage done to the environment by European countries during the industrial revolution. Recently there has been a more positive attitude to the rain forests by these governments. Currently policies include:

- developing profitable farming which is sympathetic to the environment. Rubber tapping provides an income without destroying a single tree. At present this is small scale but could be developed.
- harvesting forest produce such as fruits, nuts, honey etc.
- harvesting plants which provide medical drugs.
- developing eco-tourism which provides an income and also improves people's knowledge about the rain forest.
- sensible logging methods which provide for timber replacement not just extraction.
- creating ecological reserves where no deforestation is permitted at all.

Stop and Think

Would you rather remain poor and save the world or be allowed to become more wealthy at some cost to the environment? This is the question that has faced Brazil, and some other countries, for years.

Land use conflicts in National Parks

This question refers to National Parks in the United Kingdom only. Britain is only a small island and is very crowded. National Parks contain what are regarded as being the best areas of the countryside and since 1946 they have been protected from further development by law.

You will need to learn the details of one area in order to show that many different groups want to use these areas for different reasons. This is the theme of this section.

Look at the map opposite. Learn the main parks and be careful to use **only** these areas in your answer.

Hints and Tips!

Some areas that show the problems of conflict between users are not National Parks. Learn one case study that is a National Park to ensure that you give the correct answers.

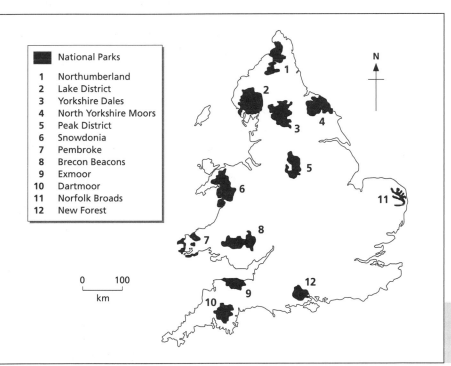

National Parks

1. Northumberland
2. Lake District
3. Yorkshire Dales
4. North Yorkshire Moors
5. Peak District
6. Snowdonia
7. Pembroke
8. Brecon Beacons
9. Exmoor
10. Dartmoor
11. Norfolk Broads
12. New Forest

0   100
km

◀ *Figure 4.5 National Parks in England and Wales*

Know your case study

Dartmoor National Park

The National Park covers Dartmoor itself (52 sq. km) and the surrounding area, from Okehampton in the north to Ivybridge in the south, from Bovey Tracey in the east to Tavistock in the west. The total area is 954 sq. km.

It is important to remember that more than 30,000 people live in this area. Their businesses and livelihoods must be allowed to prosper otherwise the countryside will become a dead museum. Included in that number are:

- **The army:** There are several military training ranges within the park. For example, the Okehampton and Willsworthy Ranges. Today's shells from tanks can travel further than 1 mile so large, open spaces are needed. The army needs rugged landscapes to train the infantry and tank crews. The Willsworthy Range includes hills above 450 m.

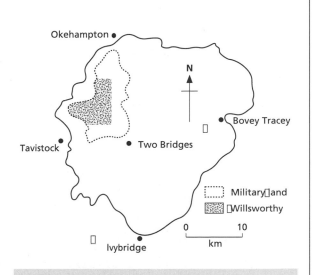

▲ *Figure 4.6 Dartmoor National Park*

Case study *continued*

- While acknowledging the damage incurred by its heavy vehicles the army claims that ownership of the land preserves the landscape by restricting public access and cutting down on footpath erosion. An army conservation group meets regularly to consider the ecosystem when planning military manoeuvres.
- Map evidence of army use includes 'firing ranges', 'danger area' and restricted roads open on certainly days only.
- **The RAF**: Pilots need to practise low flying to be able to fly under enemy radar. Fast low-flying jets are noisy and frighten animals.
- **Farmers**: High rainfall and strong winds result in harsh conditions on the higher ground. Grazing is the largest agricultural land use here. Cattle and sheep graze on the moors. Farmers using military land are restricted as to how much grazing is possible to protect the appearance of the land and the balance of natural plants.
- **Mining companies**: At Lee Moor on the southwest border, there is a significant kaolin (china clay) working. The china clay is extracted by high-pressure hose, and then it is extracted from settling tanks. Waste tips stand out against the landscape.
- **Tourists**: Summer holidays attract thousands to the countryside. This creates congestion in the narrow lanes and villages, and parking problems in the attractive areas called 'honeypots'. Footpaths and the surrounding strips of land are often badly eroded. Sadly, geographers are part of the problem (and a valid exam answer). Look at Figure 4.7. Note the damage to the grass. How many school parties can you see? All tourists need to remember that the land in the countryside is someone's property and tourists do not have free access there. Public rights of way are paths where the public can walk, but they do not give legal right of access to the land either side of the paths.
- Most National Parks including Dartmoor are high land and therefore high rainfall areas suitable for **reservoirs**. Creating reservoirs means a loss of land but some say that the lakes add to the attraction of an area. In the Dartmoor area, there are eight reservoirs.
- **Conservationists**: There are three National Nature Reserves on Dartmoor and 35 Sites of Special Scientific Interest (SSSIs). Conservationists work hard to win public support to protect these areas which include threatened rare plants, butterflies and so on. One SSSI is part of the Willsworthy military training ground and the army ensures its survival.

Stop and Think

The army states honestly that 'conservation takes second place to military considerations on land owned by the Ministry of Defence'. Do you think this is a correct viewpoint? What are your reasons?

◀ *Figure 4.7 Footpath erosion caused by tourists*

Strategies for conservation

National Parks have a legal duty to attract people as visitors but also to preserve the landscape – a contradictory situation. Possible solutions include:

1. Manage the tourists. Provide car parks that are wisely located and screened by trees. Create footpaths that keep people away from environmentally sensitive areas. Widening roads and building massive car parks are not seen as the answer as this only encourages more tourists.
2. Provide good local bus services (for example, the Lake District's Mountain Goat minibus service) to encourage people out of their cars.
3. Educate the public about good behaviour in the countryside including the Country Code.
4. Rebuild footpaths, adding flagstones if necessary even if this alters the appearance of the footpath. Purists will dislike the stone but it is a necessity in very popular areas.
5. Replant badly eroded areas and even restrict public access while this is going on.
6. Develop other areas, for example, Areas of Outstanding Natural Beauty (AONBs) and country parks to take some of the pressure off National Parks.

Hints and Tips!
Look up the Country Code but there is no need to learn it.

In the past, businesses have been very restricted within National Parks and expansion has not been encouraged. Today, the mood is changing with a growing realisation that the countryside must be a living, thriving place. The people in the National Parks actually make it work so they need to be encouraged to stay and run their businesses with fewer restrictions than in the past.

Causes and effects of pollution of a river, lake or sea

In the past all sorts of chemicals and waste were dumped in the sea on the principle of 'out of sight, out of mind'. These days we are more educated and concerned about what happens to the polluted material once it has been dumped. Perhaps 80% of all disease is water related, and possibly 50 million people die every year from water-borne disease.

You will need to learn one case study of your own from anywhere in the world. Bear in mind the following:

- **Sewage** Sewage in water → broken down by bacteria → bacteria use up oxygen in water → sewage turned into nitrates by bacteria → algae grows in water due to nitrates → blocks sunlight → river can die.
- **Fertilisers** Fertilisers from fields can be washed into streams and rivers and later consumed by people. Excessive nitrate levels can lead to health problems. This is one reason why some environmentalists prefer organic farming, as no artificial chemicals at all are used.
- Dumped nuclear waste, industrial chemicals and oil can all end up in the sea.

Know your case study

The North Sea

- This body of water is partially enclosed making it difficult for the sea to wash away any pollution. What is put into the North Sea tends to stay there for a long time.
- There are several major rivers, for example, the Thames, Humber, Tees and the Rhine, which hourly add to the pollution of the North Sea as all these rivers pass through industrial areas. The Rhine contributes about 50% of the pollution, British rivers are responsible for about 20% in total.

Causes of sea pollution	Effects
Agricultural run off	• Nitrates and phosphates lead to an increase in microscopic plants (algae) in the water. • Algae use up oxygen. • Fish and other sea creatures die. • Any pesticides reaching the sea can kill small creatures, not the intended pests in the crops.
Industrial waste	A reduction in whales and dolphins which were present in this body of water. Waste metals can affect the kidneys and other vital human organs.
Untreated sewage 300 million gallons a day – just from Britain!	Unpleasant to look at and swim in. Causes stomach aches, infections and also typhoid and salmonella. Hepatitis and even polio are possible long-term consequences.
Oil pollution • Deliberate washing of ship tankers (illegal). • Ship colliding or running aground • Spills from oil rigs. Possibly 400,000 tonnes of oil is spilled each year.	Oil coats the feathers of birds and prevents them from flying. They therefore die. Fish are killed. Oil affects plankton. Beaches are ruined for at least a year. Tourist trade is badly affected.

An alternative named example could be a specific river.

Remember there are rarely more than 7 marks for a named example so select the most important 6 facts and be able to discuss them. Refer to page 6 for an explanation of levels marking.

Know your case study

Guadiamar River, Spain 1998

The first problem is this river's name. Learn it and impress the examiners. Try breaking it down into three sections – Guad i amar. Write it out 20 times and impress yourself!

What happened in 1998?

- A dam holding back toxic mining waste burst.
- The Guadiamar River was polluted by 5 million cubic metres of acid sludge containing lead, arsenic and mercury which damaged 40 km of river and riverbank.
- 400 hectares of farmland were ruined so all the topsoil had to be removed.
- People reported illnesses developed through drinking polluted water.
- Many homes were flooded.
- 20 tonnes of dead fish were recovered. There were fears about birds eating the dead fish and picking up the contamination.

The diagram below shows how mercury released into the River Rhine in November 1989 passed through the food chain eventually ending up in the blood stream of birds.

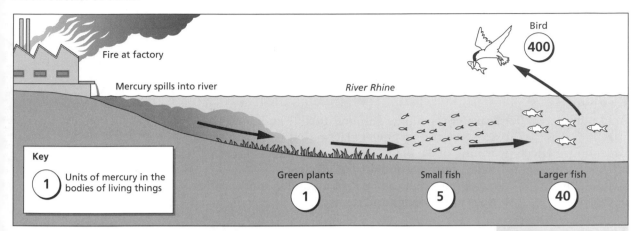

Other examples of pollution could be the River Doe Lea near Sheffield and oil tankers running aground, e.g. the *Sea Empress* in 1996. Whichever example you choose learn specific facts – say what happened and what the results were.

▲ Figure 4.8 How pollution affects a wildlife ecosystem

Examination Practice Question – higher level paper

Look at this question and try questions (a) (i) and (ii). The trigger words are *describe, explain* and *distribution*. Look at the general pattern and then look at specific types of pollution. Don't rush into the question – look at the key: a lot of information is given there. Then try section (b), taking note of the trigger words *effects, both people* and *natural environment*. You will need your own example of a polluted river, sea or lake. Learn the causes and effects of what happened.

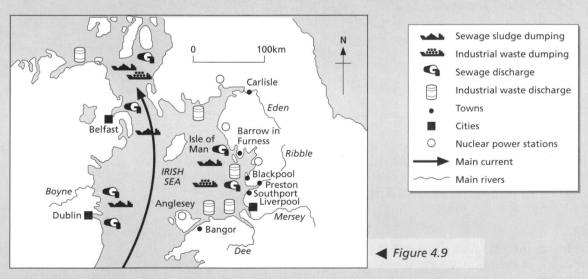

◄ Figure 4.9

(a) Study figure 4.9.

(i) Describe and explain the distribution of the different types of pollution in the Irish Sea. [4]

(ii) Explain why it is difficult for some pollutants to escape from the Irish Sea. [2]

(b) For a named river, lake or sea that you have studied, describe the effects of water pollution. You should refer to the effects on both people and the natural environment. [7]

The global environment

Key ideas
- The causes and consequences of acid rain and the importance of international cooperation.
- The environmental effects of resource and energy consumption on world temperature.

Key words

Acid rain — rainwater containing sulphur dioxide and nitrogen oxide given off by power stations, industry and traffic.

Greenhouse effect — warming of the planet due to gases such as carbon dioxide, methane and nitrous oxide.

Sustainable development — development that can be kept going for many years. It does not do long-term damage.

The causes of acid rain

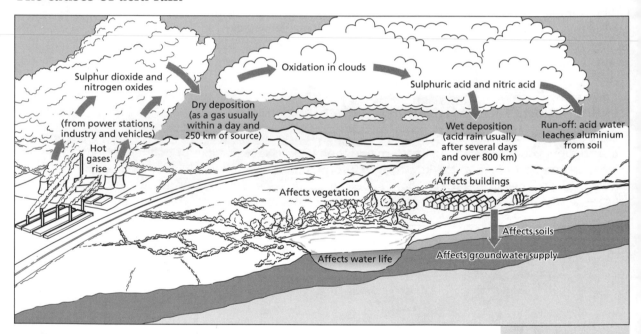

▲ Figure 4.10 Cause and effects of acid rain

As Figure 4.10 shows, power stations, industry, lorries and cars together give off sulphur dioxide and nitrogen oxide. These gases are carried into the air, either to fall to earth miles away or to be mixed with rain to fall as weak acids (sulphuric acid and nitric acid). Unpolluted rain has a pH value of about 6.

Notice:
1. The **lower** the pH value the **worse** the acidity.
2. The cause of the pollution may be in one country but the effects are felt in another.

The effects of acid rain
1. Whole forests are being destroyed; for example, Germany's Black Forest is already badly affected. It is predicted that 90% of all of Germany's trees may have disappeared by 2100.

Hints and Tips!

Do not confuse acid rain with the ozone layer problems. They are not the same and the ozone layer is not in your exam.

What is happening? The acid rain washes away valuable minerals such as potassium and replaces them with manganese and aluminium. The trees do not grow as strongly and are killed off by drought or disease which may follow.

2. Creatures such as squirrels that depend on the trees or those such as ants that live off the leaf fall are also reduced in number.

3. Fish life is threatened as the water becomes more acidic. Sweden is the classic example even though that country has only limited industrial activity. Where does the pollution come from?

4. Water supplies carry increasing amounts of aluminium. Some scientists have linked this to an increase in Alzheimer's disease, bronchitis and even lung cancer.

5. Many famous and long-established buildings and statues are being chemically eaten away by acid rain. The Parthenon in Athens (more than 2,500 years old), St Paul's Cathedral in London (400 years old) and the Taj Mahal (over 300 years old) have all survived many years with their fine stonework intact. In the last 150 years or so since the arrival of industry, much damage has been done. See Figure 4.11 opposite.

Solutions

Banning traffic, closing power stations and industry is not the solution. Choices have to be made. You do not have to make the decisions, just be aware of the options.

What are some of the options?
- More nuclear power stations (nuclear risk and unemployment in mines).
- Use coal with little or no sulphur (using imported coal, and the process is more expensive).
- Take sulphur out of waste gases, which is very costly.
- Gas fired power stations (cheaper, more environmentally friendly – miners lose jobs).
- Increase fuel prices so motorists drive less.
- Electric vehicles.

▲ Figure 4.11 Erosion on St Paul's Cathedral, London

Hints and Tips!

If you can remember the way scientists describe gases, e.g. SO_2 and NO_2 etc., it is quicker and easier. If not, then learn the words themselves.

Drax power station – an example of tackling the acid rain problem

There are no easy solutions, but Drax is an example of what has been achieved so far. Drax power station in North Yorkshire is the largest coal-fired power station in Europe. It is capable of producing 4,000 megawatts of electricity – enough for 4 million people. It burns approximately 35,000 tonnes of coal a day. Clearly this produces a lot of sulphur dioxide (SO_2) and nitrogen dioxide (NO_2).

- Drax tackled the nitrogen dioxide problem by using high-efficiency low-NO_2 boilers.
- To reduce the SO_2 in the waste gases special equipment was fitted which reduced emissions from around 250,000 to 100,000 tonnes a year. (You may think this is still a lot, but it shows that there are no instant solutions.) Progress is always in stages, not by dramatic moves. These units remove 90% of the gases, so they are quite effective.
- The Environment Agency set the maximum limit, which the power station must not exceed.
- The unit works by passing the waste gases from the boilers through wet crushed limestone, which absorbs the sulphur dioxide and becomes gypsum. (The gypsum is then used to make plasterboard!) The relatively clean gas is then released to the atmosphere. This process needs 1400 tonnes of limestone a day. Most comes from the Peak District National Park in Derbyshire. Note the problem here: if you want to ban all mining in National Parks (see earlier item) then you will have to accept that power stations will pollute the atmosphere even more. Often a compromise is the answer.

Hints and Tips!

Remember the lower the number, the worse the acidity.

Questions

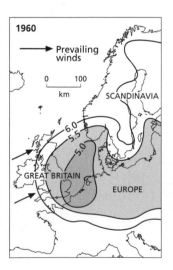
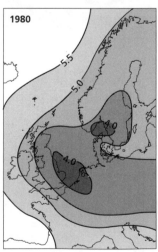
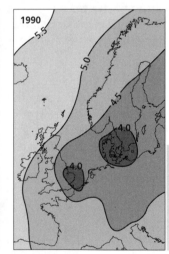

◀ Figure 4.12 Maps showing acid rainfall in Europe (pH)

1. From Figure 4.12 identify the worst area for acid rain in 1960.

2. Describe what happened to the worst areas in 1980 and 1990.

3. Prevailing winds means the most frequent wind direction. From which direction are they blowing?

4. Why is there pollution in the North Sea caused by acid rain when it isn't an industrial area?

The importance of international cooperation – acid rain in Europe

By looking at Figure 4.12 and answering the questions on page 90 it becomes obvious that no single country can deal with acid rain on its own. The wind does not recognise national boundaries. Two-thirds of Britain's air pollution is blown northeast, away from Britain but towards Norway and Sweden. French and German pollution is carried towards Denmark and Sweden. All of these countries must work together to find ways of reducing pollution. Here, the European Union can be one of several organisations bringing about change.

Global warming

The overall temperature of the planet has fallen and risen over millions of years – causing Ice Ages and times of tropical temperatures, even in Britain. In recent centuries, the planet has been warming up naturally. The great concern is that industrial pollution has further increased that temperature rise with potentially disastrous consequences.

Causes of the greenhouse effect
- Carbon dioxide is the biggest cause. It comes from cars and lorries as well as from burning fossil fuels such as coal and gas in power stations and houses. Carbon dioxide is also released when tropical rainforests are burnt (see earlier notes on deforestation).
- CFCs: gases used as propellants and in fridges are also potent greenhouse gases.
- Methane gas produced from rotting material in swamps and from animal dung.
- Nitrous oxide produced by cars, power stations, and so on.

These gases form a large layer above the Earth through which the Sun's rays can pass. This energy is then radiated outwards at a different wave length, which cannot pass through the gas layer. The heat is trapped and more incoming energy gradually warms up the planet.

Hints and Tips!
The gas layer acts like the glass of a greenhouse (which can be stiflingly hot in summer) hence the name 'greenhouse' gases.

▼ *Figure 4.13 The greenhouse effect*

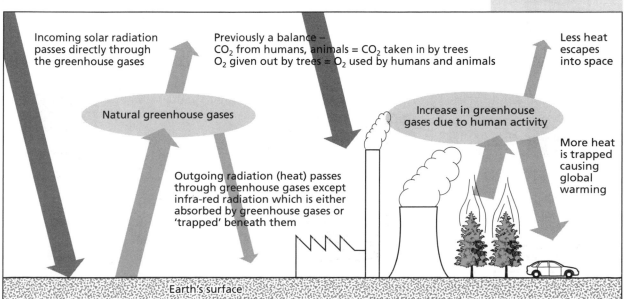

Consequences of the greenhouse effect

A warmer planet sounds like a good idea, so why are people worried?

A) Britain

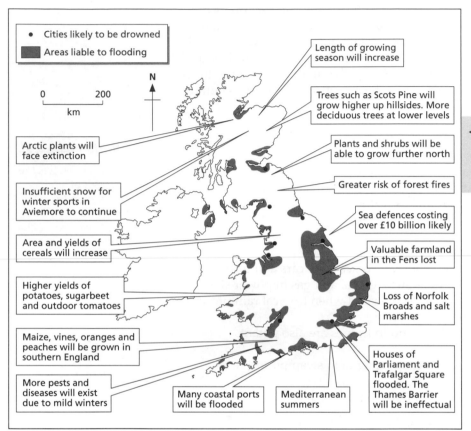

Notice that Britain would be warmer but wetter. Many of our low-lying coastal areas would be lost under the sea.

B) The whole planet

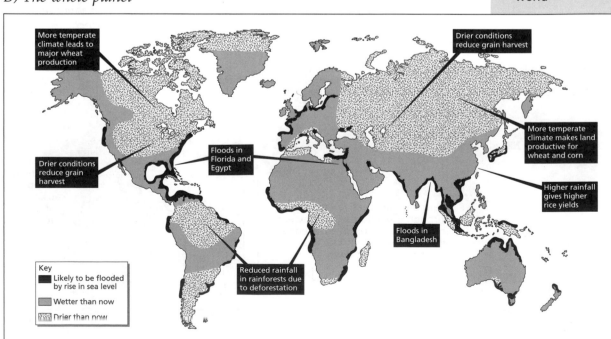

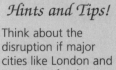

Hints and Tips!

Think about the disruption if major cities like London and important food-producing areas like the Fenlands were lost under water.

◄ *Figure 4.14 Consequences of the greenhouse effect in Britain*

Hints and Tips!

Remembering map details is hard, so pick out four effects from Britain and four from the world map. Write them down and learn them as you do so.

▼ *Figure 4.15 Consequences of the greenhouse effect in the world*

- Scientists disagree about the effects of global warming and the speed with which it will happen.
- However, a 1 metre rise in sea level by 2100 is a possibility. This would be caused by expansion of the sea, as it became warmer. The melting of the polar ice may also lead to a rise in sea level but the exact way in which this would happen is unclear. Bangladesh, for example, would be hard hit.
- What is quite clear is that there would be a shift in climate belts (this may have already started). There would be higher rainfall in some areas but less in others, especially the grain-growing regions around 40°N. This has implications for food supplies around the world.

Strategies to combat global warming
- Governments around the world have a dilemma – how to persuade people to use their beloved cars less for the sake of the planet and yet still get themselves voted back into government at the next elections!
- Governments need to try to reduce energy demand using strategies that include better insulation in houses and more efficient fuel systems in cars.
- Switching power stations to gas or even nuclear power would reduce greenhouse gas emissions. It would cause unemployment in coal mining areas but this is part of Britain's approach. The dash for gas is being followed on economic and environmental grounds.
- Developing cars/lorries/buses that use electric or low-pollution engines is also a current strategy. California sets the pace in car regulation due to its smog problems but the rest of the world follows. A hybrid car using a petrol engine and a battery-driven motor may become quite common for a variety of reasons but a less-polluted atmosphere should result with beneficial consequences for the planet.
- Find alternatives to greenhouse gases. The drive to provide CFC-free products and other alternatives is well on the way.
- Following an international conference at Rio de Janeiro, the British government tried to steadily increase fuel tax in order to reduce pollution. Many people objected and the strategy was dropped. However, owners of company cars in Britain are now being taxed according to the level of pollution caused by the car. The hope is that these owners will choose more environmentally friendly cars.

As with acid rain, it is only by working together that countries will solve this problem.

This will not suddenly happen in 2100. The process has started and will continue all through your lifetime.

Summary

Key words to know and understand

Acid rain	Ecosystem	Raw materials
Biodiversity	Global warming	Reafforestation
Conservation	Landscaped	Stewardship
Deforestation	National Parks	

Check list for revision

	Understand and know	Needs more revision	Do not understand	Refer to pages
I understand and can name areas where there are conflicts in attitudes to mining.	☐	☐	☐	78
I understand that the provision of energy has environmental consequences.	☐	☐	☐	79
I realise why the rain forest is so fragile.	☐	☐	☐	80–81
I understand what National Parks are.	☐	☐	☐	83
I realise that different groups have different attitudes to the useage of National Parks.	☐	☐	☐	83–84
I can name five groups who wish to use National Parks.	☐	☐	☐	83–84
I can describe the causes of pollution in a named area of water.	☐	☐	☐	85
I can explain the effects of that pollution.	☐	☐	☐	85
I can describe in detail the causes of acid rain.	☐	☐	☐	88
I can describe in detail the effects of acid rain.	☐	☐	☐	88–89
I can explain the greenhouse effect and its consequences.	☐	☐	☐	91–93
I can describe some of the strategies to try to reduce the greenhouse effect.	☐	☐	☐	93

Know your case studies

Which real places have you studied as an example of...
- Extraction of raw materials in an MEDC   name:_____   p 79
- Conflicts over land use in National Parks   name:_____   p 83–84
- Water pollution   name:_____   p 86

Preparation for Papers 3 and 4

This accounts for 25% of the final marks and will last 1 hour; again it will be set at two levels.

These papers test skills *and* understanding and its application.

This section covers all the skills to be tested in the exam. Work your way through and pay particular attention to the areas where you scored only average or below-average marks.

As with the exam itself the exercises link in with the work learnt in Units 1–4, so as well as developing your skills it is also a useful revision exercise. There are nine aspects to cover but they will all be mixed together in the exam itself.

The Ordnance Survey map

Symbols
You do not have to learn the symbols but time is short in the exam, so learn as many as you can and understand them. In particular:
- Red lines = main or trunk roads. Give the *number* of each *relevant* road if required to do so.
- Thick blue lines = motorways.
- Brown lines = B (secondary) roads. Less important roads generally, but note the overall pattern if relevant to the question.

The above are easy to spot. Less obvious but very important are the thin brown contour lines. Before answering any questions have a look to see the overall pattern of the lines. Are there any prominent hills? In which direction do they run? Generally how high are they? Are there any gaps that are used by the roads?

Read the examples, then try the questions. The answers are given at the back of the book.

Grid references
These are used to locate areas and features on maps. Four-figure grid references give the reference for a grid square on a map. Six-figure grid references are more accurate and pin-point a 100 metre square area within a grid square. Figure 1 shows you how to give a four and six-figure grid reference.

Look at figure 13 on page 105.

Q 1   Give the four-figure grid references of:
- The two service areas marked (s) at Strensham on the M5.
- Upton on Severn Village
- Ryall Village (opposite Upton).

Hints and Tips!
As with the previous paper, aim for full marks. Do not be content with only half marks. Refer to page 6 for details of levels marking.

Hints and Tips!
You are allowed to take a magnifying glass into the exam. This is worthwhile even if your eyesight is good.

Hints and Tips!
Use a piece of paper to copy the 1/10th of a kilometre markings shown on the scale usually found at the bottom of the map. This gives greater accuracy when giving six–figure grid references.

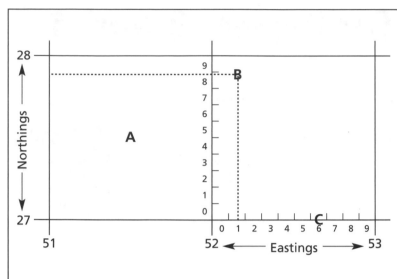

Four-figure grid reference
Give the number of the line forming the left hand side of the square (easting) followed by the number of the line forming the bottom of the square (northing)
Four-figure grid reference for square A is 5127

Six-figure grid reference
Give
• the easting (as in four-figure grid reference)
• the number of tenths along
• the northing (as in four-figure grid reference)
• the number of tenths up.
Six-figure grid reference for spot B = 521278; C = 526270

▲ *Figure 1 How to give a four- and six-figure grid reference*

Q 2   Look at Figure 13 on page 105. Name the feature at:
853 401   947 427
865 415   852 408
860 392

Compass directions

You need to know the eight points of the compass but try to understand all 16 if you can. Read question 3 carefully. Is it direction from place A to place B, or to place A from place B?

Look at Figures 1 and 13.

Q 3   Give the direction:
• from Upton upon Severn to Ryall
• and to Ripple village (87 37) from Upton upon Severn

Notice the difference in the wording of the question.

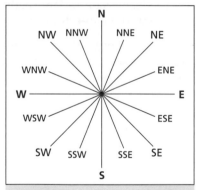

▲ *Figure 2 The 16 points of the compass*

All OS maps have north at the top.

All grid squares on OS maps measure 1 square kilometre – use to estimate distances on a map and as a check that the distance you have measured accurately is sensible.

Distances

This question develops your measuring skills.

Q 4   Look at Figures 3 and 13.

a)   The meanders of the river Severn are different from those of the river Avon to the east. Measure the length of the river Severn between the points 858 384 and 854 430. Convert the map distance to kilometres. Work out the direct distance (as the crow flies) and convert to kilometres. Divide the first answer by the second answer. This is the meander index.

Hints and Tips!

Don't use a ruler for measuring – use the edge of a clean piece of paper. Using an old ruler is a major source of errors.

b)   Repeat the exercise in (a) for the river Avon between 923 423 and
      952 451. Check your answers at the end of this unit.

When following the course of the river measure the short stretches of
straight river moving from curve to curve. Put an F at the finishing
point. Read off the distances from the 0 on the scale line. Use the small
marking left of the 0 to work out the 1/10 of a km.

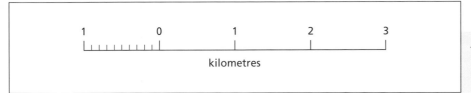

◀ *Figure 3 The linear
scale on a 1:50 000
map*

Triangular graphs

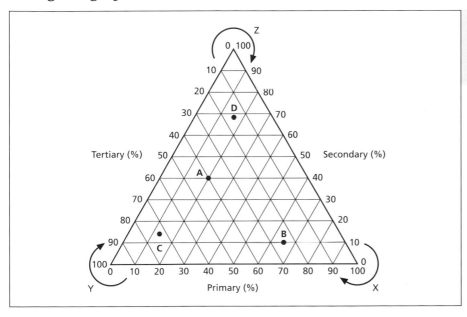

◀ *Figure 4 Triangular
graph showing
employment patterns
in four towns*

These look fearsome and complicated to start with, but once you have
mastered them they are easy and even quite fun. The great feature about
them is that you can check your answer in the exam room and make any
adjustments, then you know you have got it right.

To work out the percentage of people in primary employment in town A:
- Look to see where 0% is on the primary side of the triangle.
- Go round the corner of the triangle as shown by the arrows.
- Lay your piece of paper along the line shown Y–Z.
- Move your piece of paper across the page until you come to the dot of
  town A.
- Read off the primary percentage.

To work out the percentage of secondary employment:
- Find the 0% of secondary.
- Move around the corner to the X–Y line.
- Place your paper on the X–Y line.
- Move up the graph following the correct lines until you reach town A.
- Read off the percentage.

Do the same for tertiary employment.

These graphs look complicated because the lines are going in three directions, but take the trouble to follow the instructions step by step and all will become clear. You will need a strip of paper to guide you.

Now do the same for tertiary.

Your answers should be 20% primary, 40% secondary and 40% tertiary.

Work out the percentages for towns B, C and D. Do they all add up to 100%? If not, try again.

Reading maps

Salisbury

Study Figure 14 on page 106.
Q 5   Look at the direction of the River Wylye valley. As with all map questions of this type, note and use the general direction of (a) the river and (b) the valley.
   (c)   Notice what is missing from near the river itself.
   (d)   Look at the general height and alignment of any road or railway.
   (e)   Look for one or more contour lines between the road/railway and the river. This tells you the road and railway are probably above the flood plain and why these communications were built where they were. The road and railway builders obviously took the easiest routes – along the river valleys. Minor roads and tracks often go over hills – these were begun as tradeways in early times.

Q 6   Write out and complete the following:

The river Wylye and its valley run in a _____ to _____ direction. The river is straight in the southern part of its course but _____ in the more northerly squares.
Immediately on either side of the river there are no _____ _____: this indicates _____ land. There are no _____, h_____ or electric p_____ indicating that this area is often wet and could easily flood. The most likely use is _____.
The railway line to the west of the river follows the _____ metre contour all along the valley. The A26(T) follows the river on the east side at around 50 metres. There are 3 spot heights on this road giving readings of 63, 57 and 58 metres above sea level.
The A360 to the east is different in that it runs along the top of the hills at a height of 110 metres in box grid references _____ and _____. Perhaps this route was safer than the one in the valley as it was easier to defend. This was important hundreds of years ago.

Cross-sections
These are easy to do in theory but require very careful attention to detail, especially regarding the thin brown contour lines.

This question is worth 7–8 marks but is time-consuming, so be careful in the exam not to spend to long on it.

Always use strips of paper, never a ruler. If paper is not provided use the edge of your exam paper. Be accurate.

Sometimes half of the cross-section is provided on the answer sheet – make sure you link up correctly with what is provided.

Ensure you do not get your cross-section back to front.

> Q 7   Using the Salisbury map on page 106, draw a cross section from
>   X to Y starting at the railway at 086 334. Mark on the A36(T), the
>   river Wylye and the railway. The cross section has been started
>   for you.

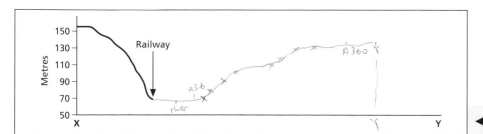

◀ *Figure 5 Cross-section*

Guidance
- Place a piece of paper along the X-Y line on the map.
- Mark the start with X.
- Mark the finish with Y.
- Mark only the A roads, railways and rivers asked for and, of course, all relevant contour lines.
- Mark the contours shown on the map, then work out the rest. Contour lines go up or down in 10 m intervals. Every 50 m, 100 m and 150m line is slightly thicker to help in working out the height of the lines.
- Lengthen some of the marks on your paper to ensure clarity.
- Check your work against the example below.

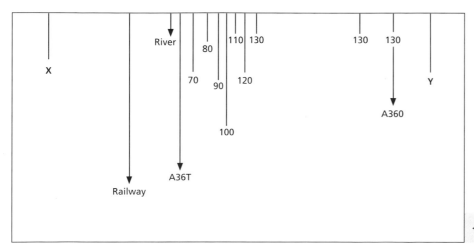

◀ *Figure 6*

You will then need to convert your work into the cross-section. Put your strip of paper below the framework provided in the exam, and check that the start and finish points match. Directly above each contour mark, at the correct height, put a small cross. Join the crosses up to form a flowing curve. Add any A roads etc., as shown below. Number each A road.

Notice how the railway, A36(T) and of course the river Wylye follow the valley, whereas the A360 runs along the top of the hill, perhaps following the route of an ancient trackway that was built high up for defence purposes. Notice also that there were three 130 metre marks. Look at the diagram below. See how the land rises above 130 m to start with, then falls and finally rises again above 130 m. Don't assume the slope will be in one direction every time.

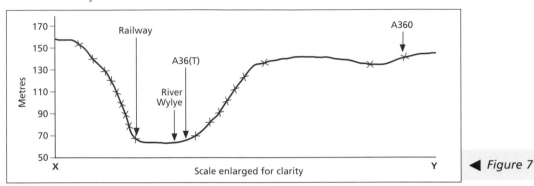

◀ *Figure 7*

Sketch plans

You may have to plot the course of a contour line or road on a grid provided by the exam board.

You are allowed to take a magnifying glass into the exam room (check this with your teacher first). Contour lines sometimes 'disappear' under words and roads. The exam board will not choose an awkward contour line, but a magnifying glass will help.

Example
Photocopy the grid below.

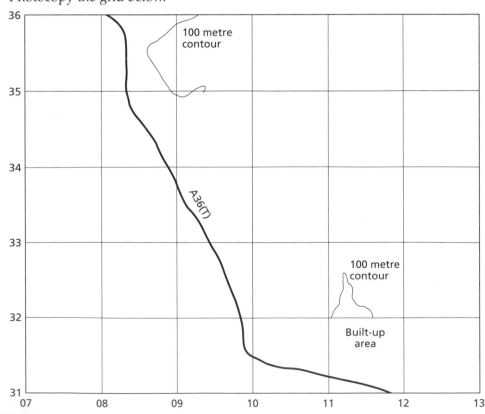

◀ *Figure 8*

Q 8   Using the Salisbury map on page 106.
  • Draw the 100 metre contour line on the grid. Be as accurate as you can.
  • Identify the correct line.
  • Check one square at a time that you are still on course.
  • Check that your contour line is in the correct place in relation to other features the exam board adds to the grid. For example, is the 100 metre contour line to the east of the A36 in the grid square 0934 and 0933?
  • Now trace your answer and check it against the answer at the back.

Hints and Tips!

The best examination answers always include specific information from the map in the answer, e.g. named places and locations using four- and six-figure grid references.

Describing physical and human features from maps

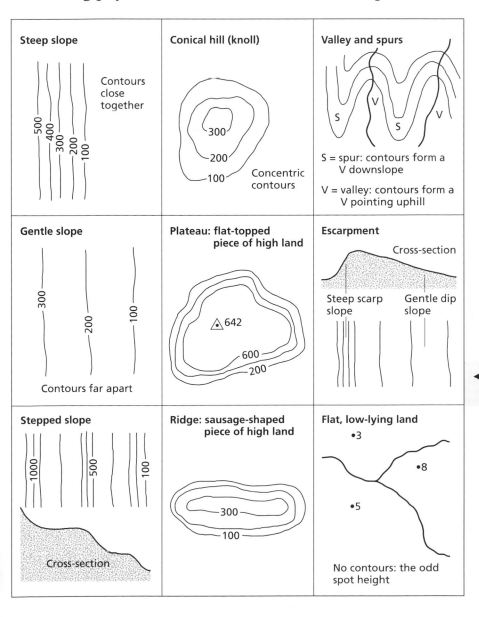

◀ *Figure 9 Simple contour patterns*

There are bound to be questions in the skills section which ask you to describe features on the map. You may be asked to describe:
- Relief – the height and shape of the land
- Drainage – the surface water features, e.g. rivers, lakes, marsh
- Vegetation – includes the obvious green wooded areas but look out for ┄┄ which means rough grassland. On the 1:25 000 map vegetation is shown in much more detail – check the symbol key carefully
- Land use – what the land is used for
- Settlement – its location (where it is); its shape (linear, star-shaped, nucleated) and the pattern (concentrated, dispersed, evenly spread)
- Patterns of communication – remember this includes railways and canals as well as roads.

Describing relief

To describe the relief on a map you need to use contour lines, spot heights and trig. points. It is useful if you can recognise simple contour patterns like those shown in Figure 9.

Check-lists for describing features on maps

Relief	Drainage
Contour patterns (Figure 1) Landforms Steepness of slopes Heights (general height, maximum, lowest) Valleys – number, shape, valley floor, gradient	Number of rivers Direction of flow Width Straight or winding Tributaries Human influence – straightening etc lakes and marsh
Vegetation	**Communications**
Woodland – location, amount, plantations or natural, windbreaks Rough pasture – location, amount	Types Direction Landforms followed or avoided Influence of settlement
Settlement	**Land use**
Site – height, slope, landform, water supply, resources Situation – relate site to relief and drainage and other settlements route focus, bridging point Shape – linear, star shaped, dispersed, nucleated	Includes settlement, vegetation and communications but also industry, recreational areas and agriculture

Cover up this page. What is meant by:
- relief
- drainage
- vegetation
- land use
- settlement
- communication patterns?

Hints and Tips!

The exam question which asks you to 'Describe the pattern of...' often catches people out.

Pattern means distribution. If you were asked to describe the pattern of settlement you need to say where the settlements are on the map and where they are not. Look for generalisations, e.g. most of the settlements are near the coast, there are no settlements on the upland areas to the west.

Satellite photos

These are becoming increasingly common in exams. They do not show how the land appears from space but the colours indicate what is on the surface of the Earth. Clouds and snow reflect the Sun's energy and show as white, deep water absorbs that energy and shows as black.

- Be observant. Look carefully for the items mentioned in the question.
- You will usually need to match the photo to a map of some sort. Try this exam practice question.

Examination Practice Question – higher level paper

Look at Figures 10, 11 and 12.

Q 9 (a) (i)   What is the direction of Liverpool airport from St Helens?   [1]

(ii) Describe the location of St Helens.   [3]

(b) Study the satellite photo which covers the area shown on the map.

(i)   Which two squares on the satellite image are linked by the Manchester Ship Canal?   [1]

(ii) Describe the differences in land use between the areas to the north and south of the Manchester Ship Canal. You should refer to places shown on the map.   [2]

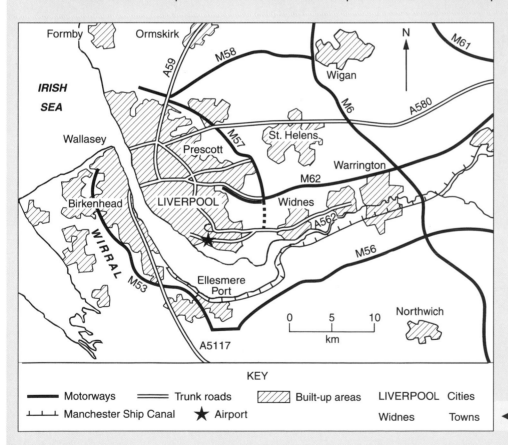

KEY

| ── Motorways | ═══ Trunk roads | ▨ Built-up areas | LIVERPOOL Cities |
| ⊥⊥⊥ Manchester Ship Canal | ★ Airport | | Widnes Towns |

◀ Figure 10

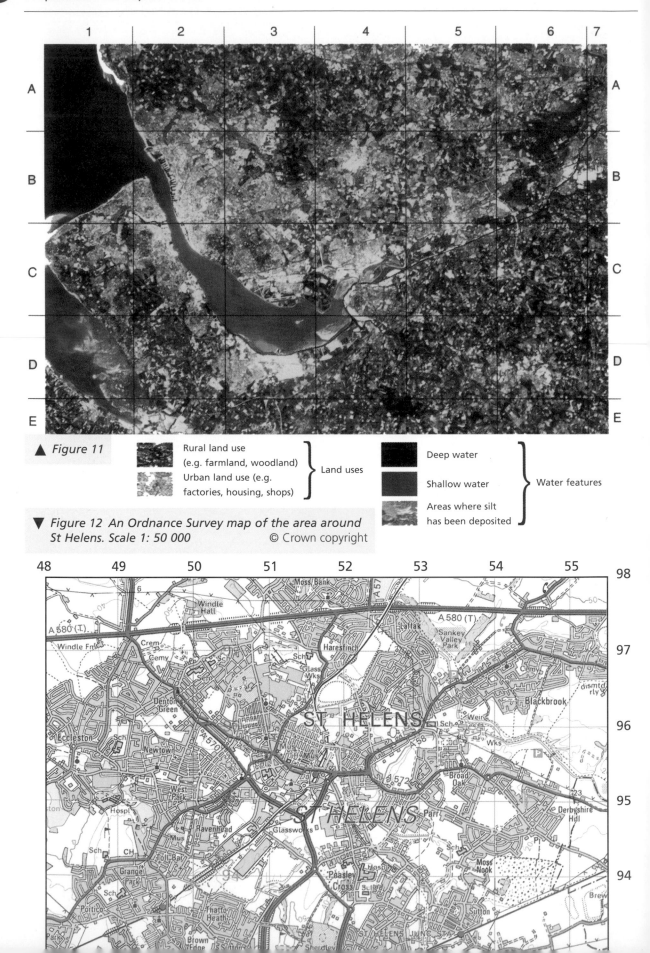

▲ *Figure 11*

Rural land use
(e.g. farmland, woodland)

Urban land use (e.g.
factories, housing, shops)

} Land uses

Deep water

Shallow water

Areas where silt
has been deposited

} Water features

▼ *Figure 12 An Ordnance Survey map of the area around
St Helens. Scale 1: 50 000*   © Crown copyright

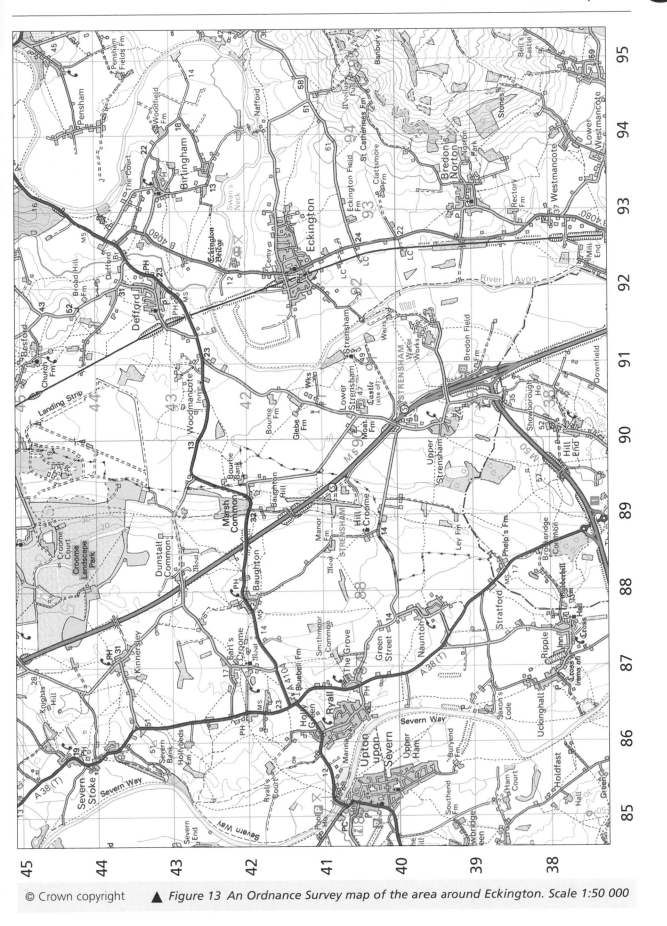

▲ *Figure 13 An Ordnance Survey map of the area around Eckington. Scale 1:50 000*

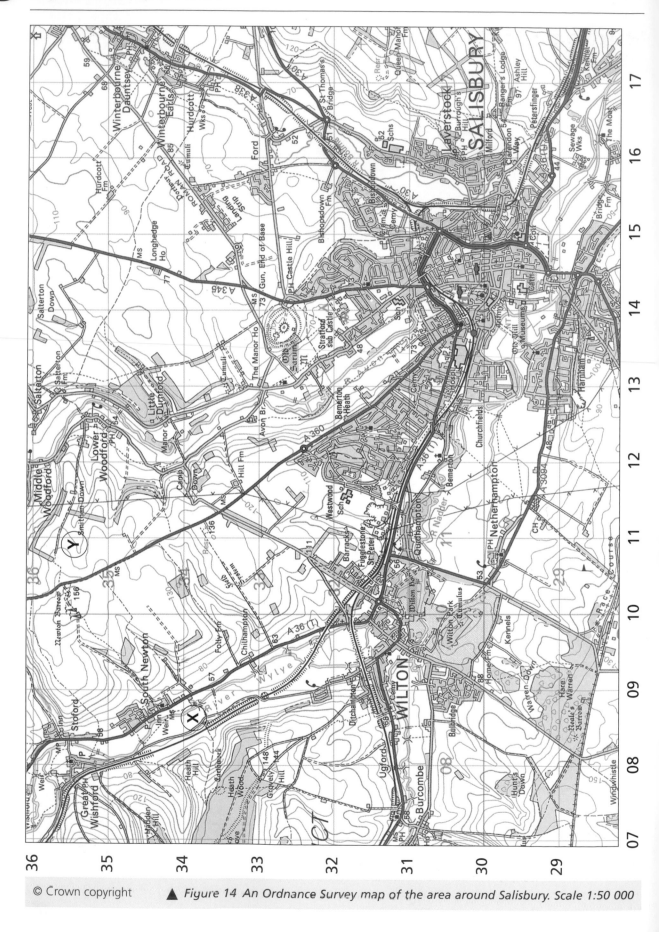

▲ *Figure 14 An Ordnance Survey map of the area around Salisbury. Scale 1:50 000*

Matching maps to photos

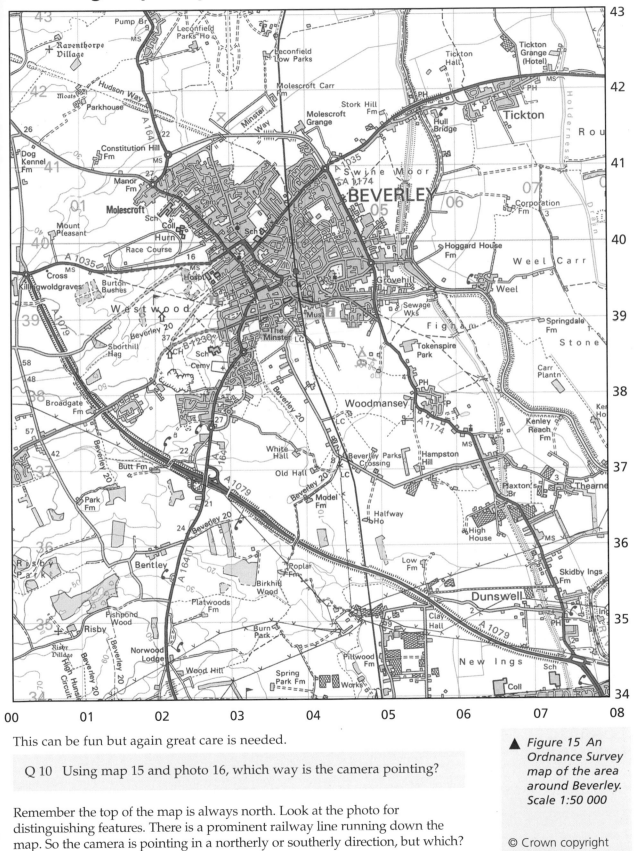

This can be fun but again great care is needed.

Q 10   Using map 15 and photo 16, which way is the camera pointing?

Remember the top of the map is always north. Look at the photo for distinguishing features. There is a prominent railway line running down the map. So the camera is pointing in a northerly or southerly direction, but which?

▲ *Figure 15 An Ordnance Survey map of the area around Beverley. Scale 1:50 000*

◀ *Figure 16 Aerial view of Beverley*

Look at the map and photo again and you will see a large church marked to the left of the railway line. This is shown as being on the left of the railway line on the map, so the camera and the map are pointing in almost the same direction towards the north.

The camera does not look directly down the track but from the right (east) side to the top left (west side) so in actual fact the camera is pointing towards the NNW.

Your exam photo may have been taken facing any direction. Always look for prominent features – road, railway etc. – find them on the map and go from there.

If the photo was taken facing south then everything is reversed. What is on the right on the map will be on the left on the photo.

As an alternative, mark N, E, S, W, on the map in their usual place in pencil then turn the map to fit the photo. Use the pencil markings to give the directions even if S is at the top of your desk instead of the usual north.

The skill of getting full marks from graphs

Look at the graph in Figure 17 and the question below.

Describe the changes in the number of houses and in the population.

Don't just say the population and the houses are going up. Write also about the drop between 1891 and 1901, the changes after 1971. Are they both increasing at the same rate? Give numbers and years where relevant.

Again try the set of data in Figure 18 and this question. What do the diagrams show about the impact of the waste water on the environment of the river? You should use figures where appropriate. (6 marks)

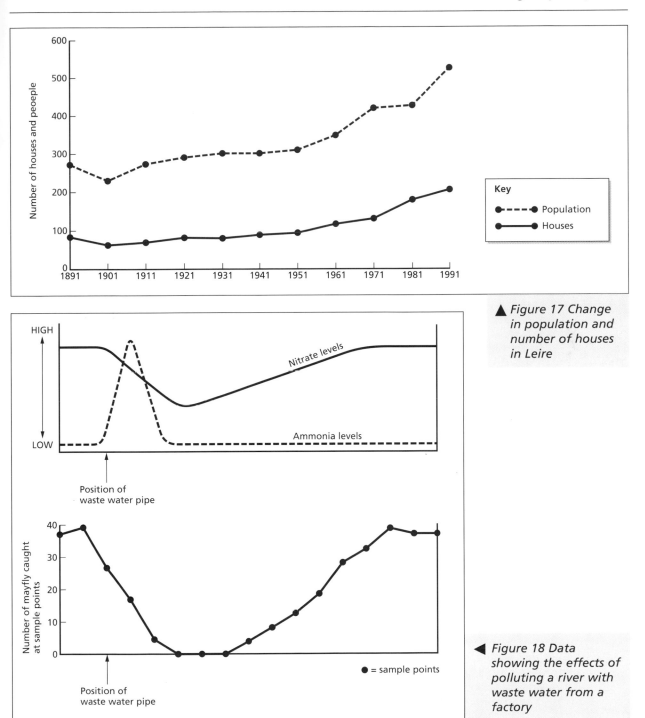

▲ *Figure 17 Change in population and number of houses in Leire*

◀ *Figure 18 Data showing the effects of polluting a river with waste water from a factory*

How do you get six marks and not just two? You write about the situation before the waste pipe pollution, the effect of that pollution at the pipe, **AND** the situation 10–16 km down stream where some sort of return to normal is taking place. Use figures as the question suggests.

Application of understanding

This question will test your ability to take information from different sources and to piece it together with your existing knowledge and understanding in order to answer the question.

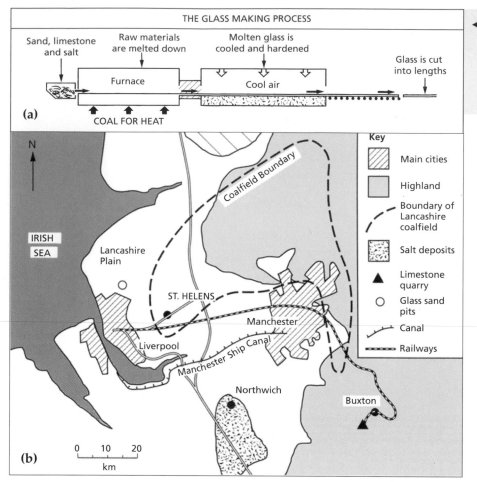

◀ Figure 19(a) The glass making process. (b) Original sources of raw materials used in the glass making industry in St. Helens

'Suggest why glassmaking was located as St Helens.' [6]

Step 1 Look at all the information provided.
Step 2 Study Figure 19 which tells you the fuel source and the raw materials required.
Step 3 Figure 19 also tells you that the raw materials are nearby and therefore the reason for locating the glassworks as St Helens.
Step 4 Look at Figure 19 again for other factors. Notice the railway line from the limestone quarry near Buxton – this is important – why? Notice the Manchester Ship Canal is not too far from St Helens. How could this help attract glassmakers to St Helens? Notice the absence of high land around St Helens. How could the nearby cities of Manchester and Liverpool help?

A Level Three answer (5–6 marks) would:
- Talk about nearness to St Helens of coal, sand, salt and even the limestone;
- Explain that glassmakers would locate near these resources for convenience and to reduce transport costs;
- Spot that St Helens is on flat land which helps the building of factories;
- Explain that the railway would bring the Buxton Limestone to St Helens cheaply and easily;

- Mention that the Manchester Ship Canal would make the export of fragile glass easier than using roads, and
- Show understanding that nearby Liverpool and Manchester helped to supply a labour force and customers for the glass.

In this example you may not know anything about glassmaking but by using the information provided, linked to your understanding of the factors affecting location of industries, you shoud be able to explain why the glassmakers chose St Helens.

Whatever questions you are given, try to include and understand the importance of each piece of information given you when preparing your answer.

Summary

Check list for revision

	Understand and know	Needs more revision	Do not understand	Refer to pages
I realise that information taught for Papers 1 and 2 can turn up in Papers 3 and 4.	☐	☐	☐	95
I understand four- and six-figure grid references.	☐	☐	☐	95
I understand the eight compass directions.	☐	☐	☐	96
I can measure straight-line and curving distances.	☐	☐	☐	96
I can read and plot figures on a triangular graph.	☐	☐	☐	97
I can draw and complete cross sections.	☐	☐	☐	98–99
I can complete sketch plans.	☐	☐	☐	100
I understand how the landscape affects transport routes.	☐	☐	☐	100
I can orientate (match up) photos and maps.	☐	☐	☐	107
I understand photos even when the camera is not pointing north.	☐	☐	☐	108
I know how to get full marks from graph questions.	☐	☐	☐	109
I realise that how I use my understanding of maps, graphs and photos will be tested.				

Answers to questions

Answers to Unit 1 questions: People and the physical world

Answers based on Exam Board mark scheme. See also page 6 for an explanation of levels marking

Page 16

(a) The two plates meet. Pacific plate is forced below the Eurasian plate. Two plates lock for a while because of friction. Pressure builds up, friction overcome, plates move, creating a jolt (the earthquake) (4 marks).

(b) San Francisco as named example (1). Many have highly paid jobs. Would be difficult to find similar jobs elsewhere (2). Always lived there. Moving away means leaving family and friends behind (2). Earthquake-proof buildings and monitoring equipment lead people to trust technology and stay (2). Belief in their own good fortune: it won't happen to them (1).

(c) (i) There were three marks here: did you name your volcano and then describe in a diagram or written form the various points on the diagram? If you did, then 1 mark for each description and the named example. Drawing a diagram would help you to clarify your thoughts.

   (ii) All trees destroyed on both sides.
   Trees caused a log jam in rivers.
   Mountain lowered by over 400 metres.
   61 people killed (all had been warned days before. Some were scientists who had come to watch).
   Melted ice caused flooding.

Answers such as 'hot ash fell into the rivers raising the temperature and so killing the fish' are worth 2 marks (an answer which is then explained). Mount Pinatubo would have been an excellent alternative answer.

Page 17

(a) (i) Plate A is moving east but plate B is moving west. Earthquake activity is moving west over the years. 1992 is an anomaly (exception).

   (ii) The two plates are trying to move in opposite directions but have become locked together. Pressure builds up and from time to time the plates will jolt and briefly continue their journey.

(b) See page 12.   (c) See page 14.   (d) See your own notes or page 14.

Page 25

Level Three answer

(a) One answer might be the Lynmouth floods in Devon, 15 August 1952.
   - Very heavy rain the two weeks before the flood.
   - Ground was saturated (full up) before 15 August.
   - 15 August another very heavy storm. Water could not sink into the ground as it was saturated, therefore it ran overland directly into the rivers.
   - At Lynmouth itself two rivers meet, increasing the chances of flooding.
   - Also at Lynmouth the West Lyn river had been channelled into a culvert that proved too narrow.
   - Small bridges over the West Lyn river trapped boulders and trees. These in turn trapped water. Later this artificial dam burst, causing a 12 m high wave to travel through the town.

Lynmouth was rebuilt to 'try and ensure the safety of its inhabitants rather than to capture all of its former character'.

Effects:
34 people died
90 buildings destroyed
1000 people homeless.

Attempts to prevent further disaster:
- Setting up of early warning system so that people could be evacuated in time
- West Lyn river was allowed to follow its natural route and not the restricted culvert route
- Bridges rebuilt spans
- Areas likely to flood in future were not built on.

(b) Flooding in LEDCs

   (i) Bangladesh

      Reasons:
- 80% of Bangladesh is on a flood plain
- Strong winds create storm surges whereby sea water is driven into Bangladesh in the autumn
- Rivers flood in summer owing to monsoon rain
- Deforestation in Nepal causes additional flooding (see Figure 1.37).

▼ *Figure 1.37*

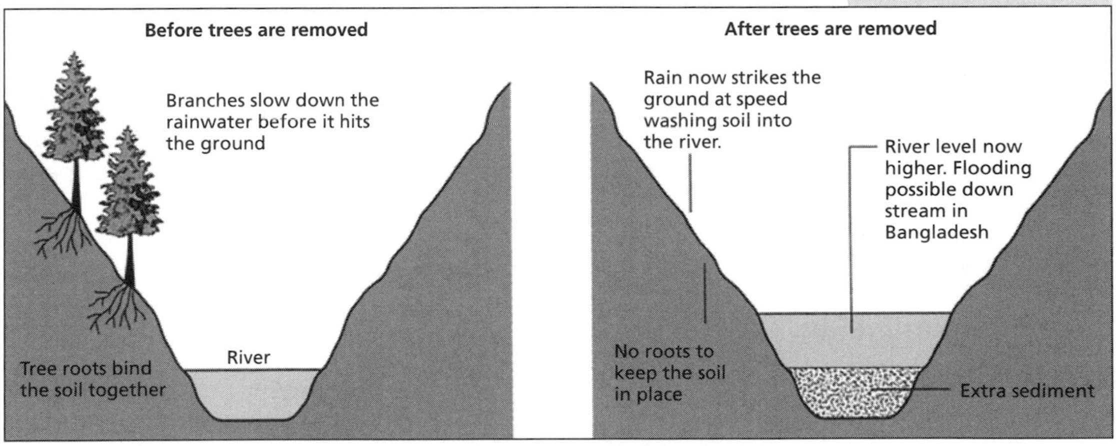

(ii) Effects:

      Many examples:
- 1991 – 150,000 drowned
- 500,000 cattle drowned
- Crops ruined
- Drinking water polluted
- Communities destroyed.

(iii) Attempts to reduce affects of future flooding

      Bangladesh is a poor country so there is a limit to what can be done.
- Embankments built to protect major cities and towns (a barrier across the whole country is impractical)
- Better warning systems now in place
- Better education as to what to do when a flood is imminent.

Page 27

(a) The slate is the most resistant rock as it is taking the longest to erode and so forms the headlands.

(b) Here the rocks are parallel to the coast. The resistant limestone has protected the weaker sand and clays for thousands of years. However, the sea has breached the limestone in places, creating Lulworth Cove and St Oswald's Bay.

     Stair Hole and Durdle Door indicate areas where the sea has again breached the limestone, creating arches and stacks which one can see today but which will one day collapse and disappear.

Page 31

Try to learn your own study in detail, but here is a sample answer.

(a) Barton on Sea – Dorset Coast

This area is experiencing significant coastal collapse owing to the structure of cliffs – sand lying over clay.

Rain water soaks into the sand but is trapped above the clay inside the cliff, leading to cliff slumping and collapse.

Sand that used to protect Barton's cliffs is now held further along the coast at Bournemouth by its pier.

The waves can now attack and undermine the base of the cliffs by hydraulic action, corrasion etc.

There will not be time to draw a detailed diagram, but a simple one might help.

Effects on local people included the loss of houses on and near the cliff edge.

The entire village of Barton is under threat of disappearing into the sea – maybe in your lifetime.

(b) Attempts were made to make the cliff at Barton more secure by:
- draining water from the sand by a pipe
- building a steel fence along the cliff to keep it in place
- placing large boulders at the bottom of the cliff to protect the base
- constructing drainage channels down the cliff
- warning the public (another source of erosion) off the cliffs themselves.

(c) Despite these measures after a few years huge winter storms overcame the defences. The steel fence has fallen down and the cliffs continue to decay. However, the boulders have reduced the rate of erosion and the drainage has added some internal stability to the cliffs. See page 6 for guidance about levels marking.

Answers to Unit 2 questions: People and places to live

Page 47 – *sample answer*

Refurbishment

Birmingham City Council, like some other councils, has repaired and improved the houses in its area. This maintains the local community, creating optimism and a sense of belonging for residents. It is also cheaper than wholesale demolition and rehousing. The Birmingham scheme is called the *Envelope Scheme*.

Using the money from taxpayers and local ratepayers, the scheme paid between 80% and 90% of the repairs to houses in certain defined inner city zones, such as Selly Park. Those outside of the zone (the envelope) received nothing. Roofs, windows and doors were replaced on a street-by-street basis, which provided an inexpensive facelift and uplifted a whole area. If the owner was unwilling to pay the remaining 10% or 20% then the work was not carried out. Trees were planted and play areas created. Why did the Council pay to improve homeowners' properties? Individual houses being refurbished would not improve or 'save' an area. A whole-area approach is needed for it to work.

Test yourself, page 52

(a) Missing words are: low-order goods, travel, high-order goods, expensive, a long way, threshold, hierarchy.

(b) High number of people during the daytime, expensive land, tall buildings to reduce need for land, land use by offices and the more expensive shops.

(c) See page 52.

(d) (i)   Takes trade from town centres and may destroy them.
(ii) Creates traffic congestion near out-of-town centres.
(iii) Not everyone can reach out-of-town centres (e.g. old and those without cars).
(iv) Out-of-town centres often have only the standard main shops. Little scope for small family businesses.

Page 54

(a) (i) 1996

  (ii) Variety of answers includes more car ownership, increase in community, more out-of-town shopping.

  (iii) Increased noise pollution, increased air pollution, traffic slower, building decay, more asthma problems etc.

(b) (i) Many routes go in different directions/network is more complete/can get to more places/serves Manchester airport.

(c)

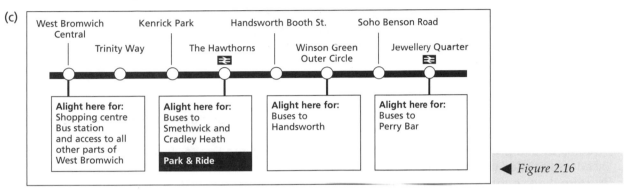

◀ Figure 2.16

Examples of traffic control described earlier in the guide and/or a particular project. Newcastle, Manchester, Sheffield and now the West Midlands have modern tram systems. Grenoble is a European example you could use. West Midlands – new system between Birmingham and Wolverhampton. Modern trams now use the route of a derelict railway line then run along streets in Wolverhampton centre. Bus services link with most town stations. Electronically powered, so no pollution. Cycles can be stored at any tram stop, and many stops have car parking facilities. Frequent service (every 10 minutes or less) and each tram carries 158 passengers.

Other answers: by-pass ring road, bus lanes, cycle ways etc. Need to name the town involved for the fourth mark.

Exam Board comment

The higher paper asked for problems of building a metro system. Some candidates did not use the evidence from the diagrams. A few wrote about problems operating the system not building it. So read each word carefully!

Answers to Unit 3 questions: People and their needs

See page 6 for an explanation of levels marking.

Page 60

(a) (i) Turkey

  (ii) Positive/negative relationships/life expectancy increases, infant mortality rate decreases. Explanation relates wealth of a country and population to levels of health care: diet; social and welfare provision; etc.
  E.g. In rich countries people live longer/fewer babies die because they have a balanced diet but in poor countries people die from malnutrition and diet deficiency diseases such as kwashiorkor. In rich countries people can be treated for illness in hospital but in poor countries babies die because there are insufficient doctors to look after them.
  In rich countries old people have better health care and services to look after them but in poor countries people die earlier through diseases which are not treated.
  Direct comparison is not needed.
  1 mark for relationship

Both basic statements together = 1 mark.
Wealth alone accepted.
Developed/developing accepted if contrasted
'Better' = Max. 1 mark
Disease 1 mark, Reason 1 mark, Named disease 1 mark,
No marks for named countries.

(b) (i)   Availability of food; tradition; money to buy food for the family; capability of country to import; commercial/subsistence farming systems; etc.
1 mark for each point but reserve 1 for each country.

(ii)   Malnutrition; deficiency diseases, e.g. marasmus – TB etc.
obesity; heart disease; inability to do manual work (subsistence farming) etc;
Underweight 1 mark/weak bone formation 1 mark
Unable to work properly 1 mark
No reserve UK/India

(c) e.g. Union Carbide factory at Bhopal, India
Environment: factory built in residential area: visual intrusion; toxic gas released into atmosphere; loss of crops and animals; etc.
Quality of life: provided jobs and training; brought money into local economy; improved some local services; satisfied demand for fertilisers and pesticides needed by farmers; attracted people from surrounding countryside to city; 2500 died when accident occurred; >100 000 injured.
Accept positive and negative effects.
Reserve 1 mark for named and located manufacturing industry.
Note the need once again to know your case study in detail.
If details were vague or the industry was not named, then only a maximum of 4 marks were allowed.

Page 65

(a) (i)   New crops of rape seed and sugar beet
More barley
New farm buildings
Hedgerows removed
Marshland drained
Fewer animals

(ii)   EU Subsidies favoured crop growing rather than dairy produce by the 1990s.
Large machines need large fields, so hedges were removed to give bigger, more regular fields.
Fewer hedges meant less wildlife.
Land drained to give more farmland.

(b) **Set aside** – farmer agrees to leave field empty for a minimum of 5 years in order to reduce production and so cut the surplus. May use land for tourism and still receive payments.

Quota – restrict amount of milk produced. Farmers are fined if quota is exceeded.

Subsidies – can ignore market price and produce as much as possible. Leads to overproduction.

Diversification – try other types of farming. Not dependent on one type and so safer from unexpected events.

(c) Commercial farming is for profit.
Subsistence is to feed oneself and one's family.

> **Exam Board comment**
>
> In (a)(ii) some did not explain the differences but wasted time describing them.
>
> In (b) some described the policies but did not describe how they affected farmers' decisions.

Page 73

a) (i) 1,210 – 1,250 million tonnes (need units)

   (ii) Pattern is summarised as:

Date:	1980	1982/83		1990	1992	1996	1997
Figures:	1000+	950		1100	1250	1200	1220
				PEAK			
CHANGE		Decrease	Increase		Rapid increase	Decrease	Increase

Allow + or – 10 for energy figures except 1980.
Details of change: 4/5 changes = 2 max.
                   2/3 changes = 1 max.

or general increase between 1980–1997 = 1 max.
Plus: two energy figures and two dates which correspond = 1 mark
     four energy figures and four dates which correspond = 2 marks

b) (i) Main changes: 2 max. for two of the following:
        coal decreased
        gas increased
        alternatives increased

   NOT: nuclear/oil

   1 mark reserve for % figs: no tolerance
        coal: 25 to 17 : -8
        gas: 15 to 24 : +9
        alternatives: 2 to 5 : =3

   Can score 3 max. by reference to % figures.

> **Hints and Tips!**
>
> Notice the need to *explain* your answers. This is true throughout the whole exam.

   (ii) Ideas such as:
        exhaustion of non-renewables/alternatives are inexhaustible; government policy; change in relative cost of energy sources; development of technology in alternatives; development of 'new' fuels – for example, gas as vehicle fuel; discovery of new fossil fuel reserves; environmental concerns of air pollution; acid rain/global warming; mine closures; lack of investment; geological problems of mining; more gas-fired power stations. Ref. to cleaner or cheaper fuels to 1 max. unless developed.

   NOT: domestic coal fires/steam trains/nuclear fears/disposal of nuclear waste/named alternatives/

   Single point marking, credit development

Answers to Unit 4 questions: People and the environment

Page 87

(a) (i) Near the coast, near estuaries, i.e. where rivers run into the sea (general answers), and sludge dumping mainly off the Irish Coast. (Specific answer).

        These are specific descriptions. Did you get any marks for *explaining*? e.g. The rivers running through industrial cities carry pollution into the sea, especially near the estuaries? (This would gain 2 marks.)

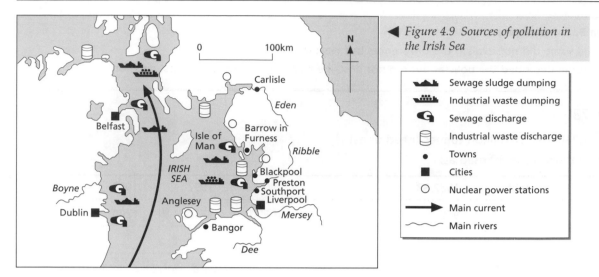

◀ Figure 4.9 Sources of pollution in the Irish Sea

(ii) The sea has few outlets. Much of the pollution is away from the cleansing main current.

(b) This is a sample answer using a case study about the Rhine (chemical released into the Rhine in Switzerland in 1989 and was carried north through Germany and out to the North Sea).

Effects on people included people banned from being near the river; drinking water polluted, water supplies had to be brought in.

Effects on environment All life in river was killed between Basle in Switzerland and Mannheim in Germany, damage for the 10 years following the incident. Animals that drank the water also died.

Exam Board comment

Many candidates chose the wrong case study from the ones they had learnt. They were not able to describe in sufficient *detail* the effects on both *people* and the *environment*.

Answers to questions in Paper 3 and Paper 4

1 • 9039   8940
  • 8540
  • 8640

2 Church with a tower, Road junction, Disused railway, Spot height 14 metres above sea level, Picnic site

Fewer than four right? Check again how to do grid references. Start in the bottom left corner of the map, move along the bottom, check all three numbers, return to bottom corner and then move up the side. Collect the remaining three numbers. Then recheck against the correct answers above.

3 • Northeast   • Southeast

4a River Severn index = 1.3 (6.2 km ÷ 4.7 km)
  b Avon index = 2.4 (9.9 km ÷ 4.1 km)

5 Look at page 95 for some help.

6 Northwest to southeast/meanders/contour lines/flat/roads/houses/pylons/grassland/60/1133/1132

7 See top of page 100 for completed cross-section.

8 See illustration on right

Hints and Tips!

Always give the grid references of the **symbol** of the feature e.g. the **dot** of the 14 metre spot height – not the number itself.

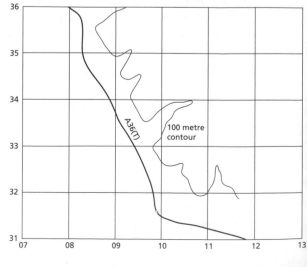

Page 103

9 (a) (i) SW or SSW

(ii) Level 3 – 3 marks – North of the M62, South of the M58 etc.
– East of Liverpool, West of Manchester, 10km from Liverpool

(*Note* named roads, accurate compass directions, use of measurements)

Level 2 – 2 marks – Answers naming just the roads *or* the towns

Level 1 – 1 mark – Answers lacking detail (or effort!), e.g. near Liverpool. Try for top level answers always!

(b) (i) C2 and A7

(ii) Level 2 answer – 2 marks – Contrast urban and rural areas north and south, e.g. more urban to the north. Include example, e.g. St Helens and Liverpool.

Recognise the exceptions, e.g Ellesmere Port to the south and rural areas in the north.

So how do you get that higher grade?

In the beginning of this book I gave you a challenge, so how do we achieve it?
- Revise. There is no magic alternative. There will have to be a few sunny days spent indoors working. What are a few weeks compared with a lifetime of success?
- Revise effectively – be smart. Be ready to give a seven mark answer. Write down five geographical facts about each of the 22 named examples, if you can. See how the facts relate to each other. Put them on a poster. Carry them with you. Do whatever works for you!
- Graphs – look at the whole graph – describe each major trend and change, give figures and years.
- Look for anomalies (exceptions). If in a map or graph question there is one town or country that does not fit the overall trend, then mention it. But do not spend the whole exam looking for them.
- Be clear about command words in the question – e.g. Describe, Explain, Contrast etc. They all have different meanings.
- Be clear about the word 'processes'. The processes of sea erosion for example are not stacks, arches, pillars etc. They are corrasion, scouring, hydraulic action etc.
- Answer the question given. Despite the pressure of the exam, read each part of the question carefully.

Finally do not be content with giving just any old answer worth a couple of marks. Two marks out of seven means five marks lost. **Go for full marks every time.**

Finally

Write down the five most important pieces of advice you have learned.

1. _____
2. _____
3. _____
4. _____
5. _____

Try to remember and follow these pieces of advice.

We wish you well with your planned revision and the exams themselves.

Index